I0037173

2020 VISION

INVESTMENT WISDOM FOR TOMORROW

HARRY LIEM

MERCER

MMC MARSH MERCER KROLL
GUY CARPENTER OLIVER WYMAN

Copyright © 2007 Harry Liem

The moral right of the author has been asserted. All rights reserved. No part of this book may be reproduced or transmitted in any form or by any means, electronic or mechanical, including photocopying, recording or by any information storage or retrieval system, without prior permission in writing of the copyright owner.

National Library of Australia Cataloguing-in-Publication data:

>   Liem, Harry.
>   2020 vision : investment wisdom for tomorrow.
>
>   Bibliography.
>   Includes index.
>   ISBN 978 0 646 48115 9 (pbk.).
>
>   1. Investments - Australia. 2. Hedge funds - Australia.
>   I. Title. II. Title : Twenty twenty vision.
>
>   332.60994

Cover design by Rob Cowpe
Layout and book production by Michael Hanrahan Publishing
(www.mhpublishing.com.au)

10 9 8 7 6 5 4 3 2 1

Disclaimer

The material in this publication is of the nature of general comment only, and neither purports nor intends to be advice. The material has been prepared without taking into account any person's particular objectives, financial situation or needs. Readers should not act on the basis of any matter in this publication without considering (and if appropriate taking) professional advice with due regard to their own particular circumstances. The interviewees, author, publisher, Mercer (Australia) Pty Ltd, and all other companies in the MMC group of companies expressly disclaim all and any liability to any person, whether a purchaser of this publication or not, in respect of anything and of the consequences of anything done or omitted to be done by any such person in reliance, whether in whole or part, upon the whole or any part of the contents of this publication.

This publication does not reflect Mercer's views on any of the investment management firms with whom interviewees have an association, nor should it be regarded as an endorsement by Mercer of these firms. Potential interviewees approached to participate in this publication represented a broad sample of individuals in the academic finance and/or investment management communities. Not all agreed to participate and all interviews conducted are included. The views expressed in this publication by the author are personal views and not those of Mercer.

CONTENTS

*To my wife and best friend Vivian and my children Alyssa
and Julian for their love and understanding*

*To my colleagues at Mercer, Anthony Lane, Garrie Lette
and Tony Cole, for their support and encouragement*

To Aristotle for life-long learning and teaching

ACKNOWLEDGMENTS

I am grateful to all of those inside and outside of Mercer who contributed their time, effort, and expertise to help produce this book. Development of this publication within our investment consulting business was particularly encouraged by Anthony Lane, our Head of Operations, Garrie Lette, one of our Worldwide Partners, and Tony Cole, our Asia-Pacific Business Leader.

I am indebted to Jane Ambachtsheer, our Global Head of Responsible Investment, for her assistance with the section on ethical investing, and to Dragana Timotijevic, our Global Head of Alternatives, for her always stimulating conversations and "out of the box" thinking.

Thanks also go to Priscilla Campbell-Wilson for assisting with the marketing and distribution effort, and Tim Gardener, the Global Head of our investment consulting business, for the final endorsement of the project.

We wish to thank the many staff at Mercer and the investment managers who reviewed draft manuscripts in the preparation of this book. Particular acknowledgments go to them for their valuable insights, detailed critiques, assistance, and constant support throughout the development of this publication. Working at Mercer has been a pleasure thanks to the guidance and support of a number of colleagues I worked closely with over the years, especially Peter Hughes, Cecily Williams, Bruce Gregor and Simon Eagleton.

I would also like to express my thanks to all individuals who agreed to be interviewed in this book.

Most importantly, to my wife Vivian and my children Alyssa and Julian, who put up with a string of lost weekends and odd working hours.

FOREWORD

In this book, Harry Liem presents investment insights and wisdom gathered from twelve extensive interviews with leading industry and academic experts. Throughout it, Harry provides linking commentary. He ties it all together in the concluding sections which consider how markets have evolved and are likely to do so.

A strong theme of institutional investment is the search for alpha or outperformance. At the same time, it seems that much of what has been marketed as alpha is being defined away as factor-based or replicable, therefore beta. Active investment managers have long battled against the erosion of alpha as their ideas and processes are taken up by competitors. The best of them are constantly searching for new ideas and new sources of information and ways to collect and process it faster to establish or maintain their advantage.

Harry is an active participant in Mercer's detailed strategic research. We have published a number of his articles as part of our program of sharing research insights with the market. This book broadens that program and takes it a step further. We believe it will assist trustees, fund staff and other investors to better appreciate where our industry is headed.

Tony Cole
Mercer Business Leader Asia Pacific, for investment consulting

Alpha (α)

Noun: 1) The first letter of the Greek alphabet.
2) A first-class mark given for a piece of work.
– PHRASES alpha and omega the beginning and the end.
– ORIGIN Greek.

Oxford English Dictionary

*"It is not the strongest of the species that survives,
nor the most intelligent that survives.
It is the one that is the most adaptable to change."*

– Charles Darwin

PREFACE

The investment industry is in evolution. The end of the Goldilocks era and the abundance of institutional money looking for a home have left many investors faced with historically low risk premiums in many traditional asset classes. Within the investment industry, both the number of competitors and the number of available instruments competing for investors' money have increased dramatically in both the traditional and hedge fund space.

Institutional clients are becoming more demanding and increasingly conscious of the concept of separating *alpha* (reward for skill) and *beta* (reward for asset class exposure), while focusing on fees and capital preservation. Part of what was once seen as "skill" is now sold cheaply through financially engineered solutions and instruments. At the same time, demand for alternative markets has increased, and expertise has built up in new areas previously deemed inaccessible or too costly to enter.

We conducted 12 interviews with some of the world's leading academic and industry experts on how they see the investment industry evolving and where opportunities remain. These individuals are very well respected in the global investment community for their forward thinking. We asked them to share their views in *2020 Vision: Investment wisdom for tomorrow*:

•   What defines pure alpha?

- What do they think of the current investment environment?

- How do they see the industry evolving?

- Where do they see opportunities in the years ahead?

- Do they consider investing to be an art, a science or a skill?

It is generally acknowledged that with the growing influence of technology and increasing number of players in the market, the search for alpha is becoming harder and harder. At the same time, new markets and instruments have evolved that participants can readily take advantage of. Only those players able to adapt themselves faster than their competitors will maintain their leading edge. The industry is in a state of evolution, and it is Darwin's *survival of the fittest* played out all over again, in an industry that still attracts many of the brightest minds on the planet.

Harry Liem
Sydney
November 2007

INTRODUCTION

After years of speaking to institutional and retail clients in both a fund manager and asset consultant capacity, I have always found the answers to the question "what do investors really want from their manager?" vary in a wide range, from merely benchmark tracking at the lowest possible cost to making money under all but extreme market circumstances. And depending on which academic theory you adhere to, arguments can be made for both cases. In fact, what may seem like an interesting *paradox* may not be one at all, as we will explain below.

In most instances, investors are quite happy to outsource their investment decisions to external managers as they do not consider managing money part of their core expertise. In return, what do they desire from their managers?

- Consistent returns after tax and fees.

- Protection of their money (or matching liabilities in the case of defined benefit schemes).

- Reasonable fees.

It is probably a fair comment that during the roaring bull markets of the late 1990s investors were forgiving on (and perhaps confusing exposure with) skill and were willing to pay active fees for what in many cases was essentially benchmark tracking in many of the traditional asset classes. The difficulty that many active equity managers still faced tracking the markets upwards – especially during periods of "irrational exuberance" – led many investors to either index their investments or abandon their traditional value-oriented managers at an extreme point in the value-to-growth cycle.[1]

It is interesting to note that the age old active versus passive debate has transformed itself into the current pure alpha versus beta factor debate, as more instruments become available and constraints are released. The paradox we introduced earlier may not really be a paradox at all, as active and passive proponents in reality want the same thing: the optimal alpha beta structure with the commensurate fees.[2] It may well be the case that we will see a more and more polarised industry of low-cost index providers on the one hand and unconstrained actively managed hedge funds on the other hand.

From a more philosophical point of view, one could wonder whether we are really able to shift the efficient frontier by as much as we would like when listening to managers promoting newly found asset classes and alpha sources.

Basic economic laws would argue that an increased supply of money will lower its price (or return). One might argue that global investors are now fundamentally mispricing risk and that the supply of institutional money currently looking for a home could potentially expect fundamentally low yields no matter what complex financial re-engineering is performed.

With all the current emphasis on alpha, it is easy to forget that investment managers do not operate in a vacuum. There are mega trends happening in the industry that are likely to influence investors' return expectations regardless of individual manager skill. This will be the topic of our next section.

---

1 To put share price appreciation into a historical perspective, a study by GMO ("The case for cash", August 2006) shows that an investment in the stock market (as defined by the S&P 500) over a 106-year time frame would have undergone four periods (1901–21, 1929–49, 1965–85, and 2000–06, which adds up to 66 years or about two-thirds of the time) where the annualised return was only 0.5% in real terms, after accounting for dividends.

2 For interested readers, Aristotle has often been attributed as being among the first to recognise in the Law of Identity that paradoxes are unlikely to exist in nature. If a contradiction is found, it may be time to check the original premise.

TWELVE MEGA TRENDS AFFECTING THE INVESTMENT COMMUNITY

The following 12 mega trends characterise the current investment environment:

- *A more difficult monetary environment.* In February 2006 Ben Bernanke replaced Alan Greenspan as Chairman of the Federal Reserve, thereby ending the fondly remembered "Goldilocks era", which lasted from 1987 to January 2006. During his time as Federal Chairman, Greenspan steered global economies into a period of unprecedented economic prosperity, and acted as a lender of last resort during many systemic crises situations – such as September 11 in 2001 or LTCM (Long-Term Capital Management) in 1998 – thereby increasing the risk of moral hazard. Investors have become accustomed to the Federal Reserve bailing them out during crisis situations, and there are some who believe that this is the main cause of the current mispricing of risk in the financial markets. Managers are finding it increasingly difficult to find value in these instruments, and central banks around the world are now increasingly taking a hawkish approach to inflation. A prime example is the fact that the Bank of Japan has decided to let go of its loose monetary policy, after 15 years of deflation ended in early 2006.

- *Global economic imbalances.* The difference between what the US buys from the rest of the world and what it sells to the rest of the world each year now exceeds US$800 billion, a current account deficit which can only be sustained if the rest of the world is willing to finance it. After 2000, foreign investors have been left less enthusiastic about US assets due to stock and bond market valuations and the uncertainties related to terrorism and war. Many global equity managers are now underweight the US and overweight Asia, regardless of whether they classify themselves as "thematic top-down" or "quantitative bottom-up". So far, Asian central banks have stepped in to buy US assets. In the absence of their purchases and removal of fixed exchange rate regimes, Asian currencies could appreciate, although it is unlikely that the Chinese government wants to be seen as giving in to US pressure.

- *Access to new markets and instruments.* Markets previously considered too small, too risky or too inaccessible are now increasingly becoming popular, such as emerging market equities and bonds, high-yielding bonds and syndicated loans. On the other hand, new instruments such as exchange-traded funds (ETFs), synthetic equity swaps (SESs) and credit default swaps (CDSs) allow managers to trade previously illiquid markets on both the long and short side and further reduce the cost of indexing. This has led to increased counterparty risk and complexity in the global financial system.

- *Increased competition.* There has been an exponential increase in the number of funds available to the investor. Within the traditional mutual fund space, the number is estimated at 8,600 in the US alone, who compete head-on with the new low-cost index providers. In the hedge fund space, the number is estimated to be closer to 10,000 worldwide, with 100 to 150 new managers introduced every month. Lured by the higher fees, skilful long-only managers and proprietary traders are leaving their fund management and investment bank employers and starting long/short and global macro hedge funds, whereby they offer their clients customised market exposure and leverage up their skill-based returns.

- *The separation of reward for skill (alpha) and market exposure (beta).* The division of alpha and beta involves setting up new solutions for mixing and matching alpha and beta, through the use of a mechanism called *alpha transport*, implemented through either futures or swaps. Alpha is constantly being redefined, and what was once considered alpha may need to be sold at a lower price as beta as new financial instruments become available in the future. At the same time, the price for pure alpha is found to be on the increase. In some cases, sources of consistent alpha may be found in the hedge fund, rather than the traditional equity or fixed-interest space, and this provides opportunities for skill transfer (or alpha transport) to some of the more traditional asset classes.

- *Increased interest in the "alternatives" space.* Faced with expected diminishing risk premiums in traditional asset classes such as stocks and bonds, alternative investments such as hedge funds, private equity, infrastructure and real estate are proving increasingly popular. Instruments are preferred with low correlation (sensitivity) to the global equity markets. Investors are adding sources of return into their portfolios and, given the current state of low but rising inflation, there is interest in inflation-linked (real) assets such as commodities, real estate, infrastructure and inflation-linked debt, accessible through physicals, futures or swaps.

- *Changing customer requirements.* With deficits for many defined benefit plans, there is an increased focus on liability-driven investments. At the same time, clients demand higher return in a low-interest-rate environment and are willing to forego liquidity, pay higher fees and live with lower transparency from their managers. Similarly, clients are more concerned about preserving capital after the fallout from the tech bubble and the sub-prime crisis.

- *Increased interest in international investing, especially in China, India and the emerging markets.* Although the home bias is likely to persist, various factors are leading to a globalisation of investment portfolios. In the case of the US, the relative efficiency of the home market as well as its valuation are oft-quoted factors. For other countries, the size of the domestic market may not be enough to absorb the growth in domestic pension schemes. In terms of the global population and consumer growth, China and India already rank second and fourth in terms of GDP on a PPP-adjusted basis, and China's butterfly effect has already been keenly felt in commodity prices, global capital flows, a relocation of business activity, and pressure on Asian currencies to appreciate. A profound secondary effect is likely as China and India rapidly move up the value-added chain. The competition for energy sources with the newly developing nations may become a major issue in the near future.

- *Changing demographics.* According to the United Nations, over the next five years the global workforce is expected to increase by 7%, or 314 million people. The developed markets of the US, Europe and Japan will account for only 3% of the additional workforce, while China and India are likely to account for 37%. Hence, there is likely to be a disproportionate amount of global output generated by these two countries. With their focus on savings and education, as well as the build up of infrastructure that maximises the use of the abundant cheap labour and undervalued currencies, China and India can continue to achieve above average and more balanced growth rates.

- *The potential for debt bubbles in several of the developed markets.* In several Anglo-Saxon markets, high property prices (according to the OECD between 30% and 50% overvalued in most Western countries) have combined with an increase in household debt levels to 100% to 150% of household income. Speculative excesses in the housing markets have led to a resulting spending boom. Even if households did not save, their wealth has been increasing. It is very easy for consumers to access this wealth through home equity loans and to use these loans for consumption or to purchase other assets. At present, debt service ratios globally have remained manageable, mainly due to low interest rates, but this may not last.

- *Increased geopolitical and commodity price risk.* The threat of terrorism and the ongoing tensions in the Middle East mean that 28% of US federal government tax receipts already go to defence spending. Continued strained international relations will add to commodity price volatility. The 1973 and 1979 oil crises were the result of political tensions in the Middle East after the Yom Kippur War in 1973 and the Iranian revolution in 1979. These were short term by nature. This time the crisis is demand driven, compounded by a lack of infrastructure investment since the 1970s. This will take longer to resolve.

- *Socially responsible investing (SRI) has gained greater currency during recent years.* Following the fallout from Enron and Worldcom, there has been increased concern in areas such as climate change and sustainability. In its present-day status, SRI may be used as a mechanism for reducing risk and represent a potential source of alpha, using indicators of superior corporate environmental, social and governance (ESG) factors. SRI also encompasses shareholder engagement as a vehicle through which investors can unlock shareholder value.

Having set the context of the current investment environment, our next section will explain the framework for the book and introduce our interviewees.

INTERVIEWS

"If I have seen further it is by standing on the shoulders of giants."
Isaac Newton (1643–1727)

We conducted 12 interviews with some of the world's leading academic and industry experts and asked them to share their views on a wide universe of asset classes, and think on a global dimension about where they feel the opportunities lie in the coming years. All have had long and outstanding careers and remain actively involved in the industry.

Part I sets out **a new investment framework** in terms of alpha and beta and costs, and includes the following participants:

Ray Dalio, Chief Executive Officer, Bridgewater. Ray is a pioneer in separating alpha and beta in terms of concepts and products, and was adding alternative asset classes long before they became popular with the crowd. In chapter 1, "Rethinking the investment ABC", Ray will discuss the alpha, beta and costs considerations involved when building an efficient portfolio through products or overlays.

Dr Stan Beckers, Head of Alpha Management, Barclays Global Investors. Stan is also a visiting Professor at the University of Leuven (Belgium). In chapter 2, "The search for the holy grail", Stan will revisit the quest for the ultimate factor neutral alpha engine. Will it be fact or will it remain a utopian fantasy?

Part II examines **the current investment environment**:

Ben Inker, Chief Investment Officer, Grantham Mayo Van Otterloo (GMO). In chapter 3, "A brave new world", Ben will examine cycles in the capital markets and apply some of the lessons to the current environment. Why is value more difficult to come by than even in 2000? What are the potential bubbles and are investors fundamentally mispricing risk? At what stage will alternative asset classes such as private equity, commodities, timber and emerging markets become mainstream, and what new asset classes will emerge? Ben will also provide us with a broader economic framework on the role of the Federal Reserve in the new environment.

Part III takes us away from the more efficient and more richly valued developed stock markets and examines the alpha and beta opportunities in **Emerging markets – boom or bust?**

Dr Mark Mobius, President, Templeton Emerging Markets Fund. In chapter 4, "The road less travelled", Mark will redefine the intensity of fundamental analysis in emerging markets as the ultimate road warrior using the value approach taught to him by John Templeton. What makes emerging markets so different, and will the transparency and governance regimes ever improve enough so that their valuation discount to developed markets disappears?

Robert Lloyd George, Chairman, Lloyd George Management. In chapter 5, "The east west pendulum", Robert will revisit his earlier theories on the balance between East and West and explain why Asia is rapidly replacing the United States as the locomotive of the world economy, returning to a dominant position it only relinquished in the late 1700s. Robert will examine the recent developments of the capital markets in the Asia-Pacific region and discuss economic growth prospects and opportunities.

In Part IV, **Opportunities in fixed interest**, we examine the state of the global bond markets and what yield-seeking investors should do given the current low real and nominal yields and spreads.

Jae Park, Chief Investment Officer, Loomis Sayles & Co. In chapter 6, "High yield or high grade?", Jae focuses on the current trend in the fixed-interest markets towards unconstrained investing and examines the opportunities in high-yield and structured products. We will highlight some of the exotic markets, such as syndicated loans, emerging market debt, preferred shares and convertibles, and also look at the sustainability of fixed-income alpha.

In Part V, **Where to for hedge fund returns?**, we seek to answer three fundamental questions about the hedge fund industry: 1) Are too many hedge funds chasing too little alpha? 2) Are they worth their fees? 3) Can they deliver on their promises of uncorrelated skill-based returns?

Blaine Tomlinson, Chief Executive Officer, Financial Risk Management (FRM). In chapter 7, "Trends in the hedge fund industry", Blaine examines the pitfalls when digging through the rubble in order to find that one diamond in the rough among the 10,000 hedge fund candidates. What is the average lifespan of a hedge fund and what are some of the operational risks? How many hedge funds do we really need?

Oliver Schupp, President of Credit Suisse / Tremont Index LLC. In chapter 8, "The paradox of passive alpha", Oliver will discuss the topic of passive hedge funds. Indexing has been an ideal method of getting low-cost exposure, especially to some of the traditionally more efficient markets. A lively debate has evolved around hedge fund indexing (mimicking active hedge fund manager indices) and hedge fund cloning (replicating returns from hedge fund factors) so as to do away with the second layer of fees charged by funds of hedge funds. Can the philosophies of alpha and the benefits of passive management be successfully combined?

Bruce Dresner and Paul Bonde, Principals at BlackRock Alternative Advisors. In chapter 9, "How portable is hedge fund skill?", Bruce and Paul discuss the options for *alpha transfer* to provide customised solutions to clients. We will look at implementation options such as futures and swaps, costs and constraints using concrete examples, and their impact on due diligence requirements.

David Winton Harding, Managing Director, Winton Capital. In chapter 10, "Is the trend still your friend?", David looks at the role of commodity trading advisers (managed futures). How have techniques evolved over the years, and how are commodity trading advisers (CTAs) gaining their place of importance?

In Part VI, **Ethical investing**, we examine the world of investments from an ethical perspective.

Dr Rob Bauer, expert in sustainability investing and Professor of Finance at Maastricht University. In chapter 11, "Alpha in sustainable investing", Dr Bauer examines whether doing the right thing boosts shareholder value. We will investigate the different environmental, social and governance (ESG) factors that may impact companies and their valuations, and also examine sustainability investing from the firm (or micro) perspective, as well as the broader climate change (or macro) perspective. What does academic literature and empirical evidence have to offer on how to best combine social and investment objectives?

In Part VII, we go **Beyond the ivory tower**.

Dr Stephen Brown, David S Loeb Professor of Finance at the Leonard N Stern School of Business at NYU. Dr Brown will provide an update in chapter 12 as to "What's new in modern finance?" We trace the history of modern finance since the concepts of efficient markets and beta first came about, and discuss important academic trends for institutional investors. We ask Stephen why so many academics are setting up quant shops and joining the hedge fund fray. What are their chances of being successful outside the ivory tower?

The interviews are followed by a **summary** looking at some of the themes that have emerged from our interviews and aiming to provide an understanding of the future of investing as viewed by our participants.

After this, we expand on **evolutionary dynamics in the marketplace**, in which we trace the path from efficient markets onto behavioural finance and the adaptive markets hypothesis and evolutionary dynamics. What does it take to be successful in the markets and dominate as the alpha male?

Having introduced our topics and participants, it's time to meet our first interviewees in Part I: A new investment framework.

PART I: A NEW INVESTMENT FRAMEWORK

1. RETHINKING THE INVESTMENT ABC

An interview with Ray Dalio on changing
paradigms in investment management

*"It is always from a minority acting in ways different from what the
majority would prescribe that the majority in the end learns to do better."*
– Friedrich August von Hayek (1899–1992)

INTRODUCTION

Faced with diminishing expected returns on equities, retiring baby
boomers (at least 76 million in the US alone), and underfunded
pension plans, plan sponsors are increasingly becoming aware that
while large-cap equities may take up to 60% to 70% of assets, they
also account for up to 80% to 90% of the variance in plan returns.
The present default option for most pension plans firmly focuses
on accumulation mode, and this option had merit and support
from the bullish financial markets up to the year 2000. Post 2000
however, trustees are gradually becoming aware that the more efficient developed equity markets to which the bulk of the money is
allocated may not necessarily be the best asset class from which to
source alpha and beta. The equity style proliferation of the 1990s
may be replaced by the need for capital preservation and a focus on
lower volatility products offering absolute returns.

While disentangling all these issues, corporations in G-7 countries are turning from net borrowers to net savers, freezing pension
plans and increasingly transitioning to defined contribution plans,
while widely debating the merits of alpha versus beta from a wider
liability matching context.

Following developments in financial engineering, a number of proponents in the industry have suggested returning to the basics on portfolio construction building blocks in terms of alpha, beta and costs, in order to improve the Sharpe and information ratios, and in this interview we discuss the reengineering of alpha and beta in detail.

A paradigm shift

An existing paradigm often prevents us from seeing new ideas. Though investors have had investing tailwinds over the past 25 years, periods of rapid capital appreciation in real terms occur much less frequently than often thought, as we have described in the introduction of our book.

In the *existing paradigm[1]*, using modern portfolio theory, asset classes are combined based on expected returns, risks and correlations. The higher expected return attributed to stocks, and the inherent home bias, carry within them a number of constraints to creating an optimal portfolio. For example, markets that have become more efficient and more richly valued at present (such as developed equity and bond markets) still comprise the bulk of most portfolios. At present for most investors, the majority of returns come from beta (generally around 95% of their risk budget), with the 5% alpha allocation being dominated by equity sources.

The *new paradigm* is likely to involve separation of alpha and beta, and new efforts to optimise each individually before settling on the best combination. Alpha may be used through a separate portfolio or through an overlay independent of beta, and the traditional distinction between asset classes may slowly disappear as increasingly equity and bond managers are adopting unconstrained benchmarks.

Hence, the future of investing may consist of efficient beta creators (such as indexers and ETFs) and alpha generators who will compete for the whole spectrum. In that sense, the line between traditional equity and fixed-income managers on the one hand,

---

1 In *The Structure of Scientific Revolutions* (1962), Thomas Kuhn asserts that, contrary to popular belief, typical scientists are not objective and independent thinkers. Rather, they are conservative individuals who accept what they have been taught and apply their knowledge to support existing theories. As a result, scientists ignore new research that might threaten the existing paradigm.

1. RETHINKING THE INVESTMENT ABC

and hedge fund managers on the other hand, may blur in the near future as everybody starts to compete for the same opportunities.

Introducing Ray Dalio

In an era where Julian Robertson and George Soros have left the scene, Ray is one of the largest global macro money managers still standing. A baby boomer himself, Ray has been trading since the age of 12, buying and selling stocks while caddying at the local golf course. After graduating from Harvard Business School with an MBA in finance and with two years of work experience, Ray founded Bridgewater at the age of 25 in a spare bedroom in his apartment on East 64th Street in New York, specialising in managing credit and currency exposure. Ray remains Bridgewater's Chairman and Chief Investment Officer today, and Bridgewater has evolved into one of the largest global macro players worldwide.

The concept of alpha/beta separation was introduced by Ray over 17 years ago, but it was only after 2000, as equity markets corrected, that the idea increasingly gained traction. We talk to Ray about alpha and beta, as well as some of the deeper currents that move the markets.

Ray, can you define for our readers what you consider as "pure alpha"? What defines to you the ultimate alpha engine? Is it a lack of factor bias, or the sustainability of the uncorrelated alpha sources over time, or something else?

As you know, alpha is the return that comes from winning managers taking money from losing managers in a competition that is zero-sum. This zero-sum competition is much the same as a race, or most competitions, in that there are better and worse. So alpha being zero-sum does not mean an individual manager's returns are zero-sum. On the contrary, as with most competitions, in the competition for alpha there are some consistent winners and losers. And, as with most competitions, the winners are better because they work harder, devote more resources to the effort and/or are more talented than their competitors.

"Pure alpha" comes solely from one's ability to better assess what's good to buy and sell than most other market participants. Since we are equally willing to be long or short any market or market spread (that is, any beta) based on whether it is cheap or expensive, pure alpha returns are uncorrelated with any beta. We don't want to have betas in our return streams because they have relatively low returns relative to their risks relative to our alphas. Therefore, in addition to being uncorrelated with betas, pure alpha should have a higher return-to-risk ratio than any betas.

In my opinion the ultimate alpha engine has to produce lots of good, uncorrelated alphas. So it must be based on:

1) *Deep and logical understandings of several markets* (so that one can understand what's cheap); and

2) *A sound understanding of portfolio construction and risk management* to properly bring these alphas together into a portfolio of them.

As mentioned, because I believe that "betas" and "factors" are destined to have low or nil alphas relative to their risks (because making exceptional returns can't be as simple as doing the same thing over and over, and because everything becomes both cheap and expensive at times), my ultimate alpha engine has none of them in it. Also, because I believe that all criteria for investing (that is, good betting strategies) should have a logic that isn't time specific, *I believe that the alpha generators that make up the ultimate alpha generator should be timeless and universal.* By that I mean that they should have worked over very long time horizons and in all countries' markets.

You're well-known for jotting down trading rules on yellow pads, which eventually became the blueprint of your trading system. Are you still doing that?

Yes, though the process happens much more efficiently than it used to. In the past, from the point of thinking of a trading rule to testing it took a long time (to gather the data and test it), so that it was the exploration of a concept which bottlenecked my progress. Now, it's the opposite – the gathering and processing of the data is so fast that my intellectual ability to process the information is the bottleneck. The game of investing has gotten much more sophisticated since I started jotting my rules down on yellow pads!

One of the theories you suggested was the post–modern portfolio theory (PMPT).² Has the idea gained further traction within the academic or broader investment community?

The PMPT is based on my belief that the best way to construct a portfolio is to independently create optimal alpha and optimal beta mixes and then combine them. Since alphas and betas can be hedged away or taken on, and they can be engineered to be larger or smaller (synthetically), one can create very well diversified alpha and beta portfolios made up of return streams that are chosen because of their attractiveness, unbiased by whether their betas and alphas are in the same asset classes. Approaching portfolio construction this way can roughly quadruple investors' risk-adjusted returns.

Extremely rapid progress is being made on creating the optimal alpha piece of this now. In fact, it is probably the hottest thing now going on in investing. I believe that when the alpha restructuring is largely completed, investors will turn their attention to creating the optimal beta piece with the same zeal. Then the PMPT process will be complete. Currently we are running optimal beta portfolios for about 40 clients; many more clients are exploring it and we are now seeing other managers come out with copy-cat products. So, the optimal alpha piece of PMPT is very rapidly being adapted, and the optimal beta piece is being applied in a number of cases and it is being broadly discussed. I expect that in another five years or so, the PMPT approach will be pretty standard and the traditional approach will be considered pretty archaic.

Ray, the following table shows some of the main characteristics of alpha and beta, as indicated by you.

---

2 In traditional modern portfolio theory, riskier assets are expected to have higher expected returns, and portfolios are optimised according to the efficient frontier. In post–modern portfolio theory (PMPT) all asset classes are leveraged up or down to generate the same return (for example, 10%), and correlations become the main distinguishing factor. In terms of pure beta creation, using the PMPT one could potentially lift the Sharpe from 0.20–0.30 for a typical default portfolio to 0.60–0.70 for the same risk level, while minimising drawdown. For a more detailed explanation we refer readers to an article by Ray: "Engineering targeted returns and risks", Bridgewater, December 2005.

Alpha

- Alpha sources are numerous and uncorrelated.

- Alpha is a zero-sum game, and there are transaction costs and fees.

- The rewards for choosing the right manager and alpha stream are large.

Beta

- Betas are limited in number.

- Betas are relatively correlated with each other.

- Excess returns are relatively low compared to excess risks.

- Betas are reliable over long time horizons.

You mention that sources of beta are more limited while sources of uncorrelated alpha are relatively limitless, which is why you want to get the maximum number of alpha sources for diversification.[3] What kind of information ratio is possible for the ultimate alpha engine, and would, for example, 10 to 15 sources get you most of the benefit?

The answer to this question depends on the information ratios of each alpha and correlations of your alpha sources. However, if they are uncorrelated, one will get an improvement in the average information ratio by a factor of 4 to 5 with the first 15 to 20 alpha sources. For example, if the average information ratio is 0.30, then with 15 to 20 of them that are uncorrelated, it will rise to between 1.0 and 1.5.

When do you decide to turn alpha sources on and off?

To be clear, we don't turn them on and off and on again in the sense that we selectively use them. An alpha source is a betting strategy

---

3 Bridgewater targets over 100 sources of alpha, with on average 70 bets outstanding at any one time.

so that, built into it, is the size of the bet to make, so it will shut itself off if there is no mispricing to take advantage of. So, when you say turn it off, I assume you mean abandon the strategy. We do this when either, a) its actual performance is inconsistent with the performance expectations we set for it, or b) we have reason to believe that it won't work or some other version of it will work better.

Overlays offer some benefits; for example, flexibility in terms of tailor-made solutions, such as mixing and matching alpha, beta and risk constraints. On the other hand, it creates more operational complexity than a product. In general, what would your alpha advice be: access it through a product or through an overlay?

If unconstrained, for each investment manager there is only one optimal alpha portfolio. So, if the investor is looking for the manager's best alpha, and the manager only will accept assignments that allow him to create his best alpha, then his one standardised product would be both best and easiest.

Customisation is only required if the client has restrictions on what they allow. The way we work is to offer clients whatever betas they want, which we passively replicate and then we overlay pure alpha on it, tailoring its volatility to their preference.

In terms of risk budgeting, what would you consider as reasonable in terms of alpha/beta risk percentage allocation (from the current 95%/5%)?

That depends on the confidence the investor has that he can pick successful managers, what the information ratios of those managers are, and whether the investor can start to balance their managers' alphas better than they are currently doing.

Generally speaking, we have observed that most of our clients have, on average, picked winning managers, with information ratios on average at around 0.2 to 0.3, but they have been very poorly combined because they were determined as by-products of the asset allocation decision. For example, we typically see that most of their exposure is to big cap equity managers, where it has proven toughest to add value, because that's where they have most of their beta. So, their combined alphas have typically had information ratios of about 0.5.

2020 Vision: Investment Wisdom for Tomorrow

At the same time, the return-to-risk ratios (Sharpe ratios) of their beta portfolio would be about 0.4. That would imply that giving 50/50 to alpha and beta would be about right. However, if they structure their alphas and beta portfolios more efficiently, they could easily raise the information ratios of their alpha portfolio to 1.25 and the Sharpe ratio of their beta portfolio to 0.7. That would imply that they should have more of their risk to alpha than beta.

In any case, it's much more than they typically have now. Of course, as mentioned before, that depends on their confidence that they can pick winning managers on average.

You are probably best known for your bond and currency products. At which stage would you recommend a currency overlay as opposed to an alpha overlay?

I'd only recommend currency overlay instead of alpha overlay in cases where the organisation is constrained against pursuing the best strategy because they haven't yet come around to accept the separation of alpha and beta. *We have stopped accepting currency overlay accounts because they are structurally inferior to alpha overlay accounts.*

Let's talk about your investment philosophy:[4]

1) A deep understanding of the fundamentals so that pricing inefficiencies can be identified.

2) Focus: the capacity to think conceptually and independently and stand against the crowd.

3) Perspective without data mining.

4) Strategy: understanding probabilities, statistics and money management principles.

5) Substantial resources: technology has widened the gap between resource-rich and resource-constrained players.

Correlations sometimes reverse too; for example, the stock bond correlations while in general are positive sometimes turn negative. How do you handle that?

---

4 As taken from *The Global Investor Book of Investing Rules*, Harriman House (2002).

Correlations are unstable for logical reasons because the markets move for logical reasons. For example, when inflation volatility was high relative to the volatility of growth expectations, it made sense for stocks and bonds to be positively correlated, yet when growth expectations are volatile relative to inflation expectations, it makes sense for stocks and bonds to be negatively correlated. For this reason, we don't assume stable correlations, we look at a range of past correlations to stress-test our portfolio based on different correlation assumptions and we structure our portfolios to have no unintended exposures that would favour one type of economic environment over another.

When do you know when to revise the rules?[5]

As mentioned, we drop or revise our trading rules when either, a) the actual trading results were inconsistent with our expectations, or b) when we come up with better ideas.

You mentioned before that you try to avoid data mining[6] as you start with the fundamental economic relationships first. Have you ever ended up in a situation where you did inadvertently data mine?

Not directly because the rules were determined before the testing is done, but perhaps slightly and indirectly in that the goodness of test results can influence our expectations of how good a trading rule is. However, since we generally don't assign much weight to the indicator's tested performance in determining how much weight to put on the indicator, test results don't play much of a role.

What importance do you attach to technical indicators? (You mentioned before that you regard technical analysis as useless without a notion of fundamental intrinsic value.)

I attach no importance at all to technical indicators.

---

5 Any system reflects a set of thinking which is constantly adapted. The traditional "quant" nightmare occurs when a change in the market fundamentals results in a severe drawdown in the system which the quantitative trader then unquestioningly follows.

6 Data mining, in a negative context, can be about creating causal relationships where none exist.

Let's talk about the current markets. What do you see going forward for the major currencies and interest rates for the coming years?

I expect the US dollar and euro to be weak relative to Asian currencies, especially Asian emerging currencies, and I expect US interest rates to rise relative to non-US rates, so I expect US bonds, especially lower rated bonds, to underperform sovereign credits elsewhere.

A number of people have observed parallels to the 1970s; for example, a richly valued S&P, geopolitical tensions, the US in a protracted war, inverted yield curves, and the emergence of new powers (before, Germany and Japan, now China and India). What are your thoughts on that?

I agree – I think that the most analogous period to now was 1970–71, just before the Bretton Woods break-up, when Japan and Germany were in analogous positions to China and India in that they were cheap and growing fast, running large balance of payments surpluses (while the US was running deficits) and the fixed exchange rate was being maintained via unsustainably large Japanese and German purchases of US bonds.

What role do you see for the Federal Reserve in the new environment?

I think they will be slow to react, but more likely to err on the side of being too easy, especially during times of financial crises, which I think is likely to happen in the next two years. (Author's note: the subprime crisis actually occurred two months after this interview was taken.)

Are you still very bullish about emerging markets and currencies (in anticipation of revaluations and the shift in wealth to developing nations)?

As you know, my market views change quickly so anything I might say today will be out of date shortly. I find that I'm probably better at reacting to what's happening than anticipating it. There's a saying in the markets that "he who lives by the crystal ball is destined to eat ground glass" (laughs).

For the most part my outlook is broken up into two parts:

1) the current period in which the excessive amount of liquidity, funded by the large dollar denominated debt purchases from abroad, drives down risk and liquidity premiums, stimulates strong and broad-based global growth during which inflation pressures rise gradually; until

2) the expansion in dollar denominated debt and liquidity contracts, due to a combination of tightening of monetary policies due to higher inflation and a reduced amount of dollar denominated debt accumulation by foreigners, at which time risk and liquidity premiums will rise and global growth will slow/decline and the dollar will fall a lot.

I'm pretty sure that the transition from the first environment to the second will take place over the next two years. When exactly, I can't say, but I tend to think it will come late next year, soon before or soon after the US presidential election. (Author's note: as mentioned earlier, the transition to the higher volatility environment did indeed take place a few months after the interview was completed.) In the first environment I want to be short US bonds, and to a lesser extent other developed countries' bonds, long commodities and long emerging markets, especially Asian emerging market currencies. In the second period I want to be long developed market bonds, though still short dollar bonds against them, and I want to be out of commodities (though not short in dollars) and much less long emerging market assets, except Asian emerging market currencies and gold.

So, yes I'm now bullish on emerging markets and currencies, in anticipation of revaluations and the shift in wealth to developing nations, though I am more bullish on their currencies than their bonds and stocks. I even believe that the big balance of payments surplus countries' currencies will do well in a flight to quality, which is not typical.

What's your view on oil and commodities? Commodities are valued because of their negative correlations with stock returns. Any indication this may change?

I'm still long oil and most commodities, though much less so at these higher prices. I think that these commodities are about two-thirds the way through their moves in price and 80% through their moves in terms of time.

You once described yourself as a "moderate bear" back in 2000, expecting negligible real returns on US stocks.[7] Are you still a moderate bear at this stage?

No, I'm neutral on stocks. Back in 2000 stocks were very over-valued. After collapsing and then recovering their prices are now about where they were back then (generally insignificantly higher) but their earnings and cash flows have improved a lot. So have their balance sheets (they have lots of cash and reduced debt burdens), so they're cheap in relation to the current level of interest rates. That would ordinarily make us bullish, but the developments I expect (as outlined earlier) are bearish, so they roughly cancel out.

How long will the current environment last? What do you think are its causes and what are the potential catalysts for change?

As mentioned above, I think that the markets will gradually become more volatile until they become quite volatile some time late next year. Regarding the timing, that's just an educated guess.

What asset classes can you recommend for investors battling the current environment? (For example, nominal versus real assets, US dollar versus non-US dollar assets, public versus private markets.)

Whatever the case, you would want to avoid US dollar assets for the moment.

Let's talk about the hedge fund industry. Investors are increasingly favouring market neutral strategies at the expense of global macro.[8] What are your thoughts on that?

There are many ways to skin a cat. However, beware of strategies that convert small mispricings into good-sized returns via lots of leverage.

---

7   As taken from an interview with Ray Dalio in "A cautionary tale from a big picture guy", Brett Fromson for TheStreet.com, November 2000.

8   During the early 1990s the hedge fund industry was dominated by global macro players such as Ray. The percentage has reduced from one-third of total assets during the early 1990s to one-tenth at present.

If you look at the rolling excess returns for global macro, is the relative decline since the mid 90s[9] attributable to lower leverage, a lower volatility environment, less concentrated risk-taking after LTCM, or is it something else?

I can't comment on other global macro managers' returns. However, for us, it is not true that the returns have been lower since the mid 90s. They've been about the same after the mid 90s as before. However, they have been lower over the last two years. That has been because the markets haven't moved much and we didn't (and won't) create increased leverage in our positions to try to make large returns out of small ones.

You also mentioned before that a number of hedge fund strategies could be synthetically replicated using passive indices. Which strategies are least likely to become commoditised (that is, will be the most useful alpha sources going forward)?

I would suggest long/short equities and global macro because the managers in them do things that are more different from each other than the managers in other strategies.

What do you see as some of the other interesting trends in the hedge fund industry?

Besides hedge fund betas being replicated, we expect that alphas will be ported into other asset classes so that hedge fund managers will increasingly evolve into alpha overlay managers. I also think that there is likely to be a major crisis/shakeout in the hedge fund business when we move from the environment that we are now in to the second environment that I described earlier. That is because there is too much leverage held in similar positions that tend to do well when liquidity is plentiful and credit and liquidity premiums aren't expanding. Also, hedge funds recently have been like dot-coms in 2000 – one only has to say that you are one and you get lots of money. *As a client recently said, "there are about 8,000 planes in the air and 100 good pilots".*

---

9 Based on one- and three-year rolling returns from the CSFB/Tremont Global Macro index, global macro excess returns have come down from 20% to 30% during the early 1990s to around 10% to 15% at present.

What do you think of the current multi-strategy versus fund of funds debate?[10]

It all depends on how good the multi-strategy managers are. I'm not knowledgeable enough about them to make a generalisation.

What would you have done differently if you had to start all over again?

I wouldn't change anything. Life is a journey so the goal is to enjoy the twists and turns, not to go directly to the destination. I can't imagine changing anything, including the mistakes that have helped me learn.

What do you think makes a good investment manager?

- The ability to be comfortable holding an independent point of view.
- Constantly questioning whether that view is wrong.
- Common sense.
- A passion for the game.

What would you have done if you had not entered this business?

I couldn't say, other than it would have led me to travel to far away places and meet with people with radically different points of view, it would have been entrepreneurial and it would have been playing a game that provides relatively quick feedback.

How do you see the investment industry in 10 years time?

The investment business will consist of alpha generators and beta replicators (and firms that do both) following the PMPT model described earlier, and the alpha generators will have very smart people who understand financial engineering and are equipped with fabulous information technology. The amount of money firms

---

10 In their drive for more transparency, more frequent pricing and cutting away the extra layer of fees, institutional investors are showing increased interest in single-manager, multi-strategy solutions. Given that not many single managers may be able to specialise in all alpha sources, this has stirred up the balanced fund versus specialist manager debate all over again.

will expend in the competition to produce alpha, and the levels of sophistication that this will produce, will be commensurate with the fees that they earn, which will increasingly differentiate between the various gradations of quality. In others words, *the quality of play will increase dramatically.*

Finally – investment: art, science or skill?

There are all sorts of ways to make money in the markets. However, I believe that the best way, and the way that increased competition will drive investing toward, is art and skill systemised into science.

Thank you for your time.

CONCLUSIONS

Clearly what keeps Ray motivated is his "love of the game", which started as a teenager trading stocks and commodities. Although he no longer sits on the trading floor, he still likes passing orders, and loves figuring out strategies of what to buy and when. He rates passion and the drive to excel as the most important attributes to succeed in the business. As Ray puts it:

> *"There is a clear correlation between pursuing excellence and achieving happiness and a poor correlation between having money and having happiness. Success is a consequence, not a goal."*

When not hunting for alpha in the financial markets, Ray likes to hunt for deer using the old-fashioned bow and arrow. This goes to show that you can take the game away from the hunter, but you can't keep the hunter away from the game.

2. THE SEARCH FOR THE HOLY GRAIL

An interview with Dr Stan Beckers
on the quest for alpha

King Arthur: "Go and tell your master that we have been charged by God with a sacred quest. If he will give us food and shelter for the night, he can join us in our quest for the Holy Grail."

French Soldier: "Well, I'll ask him, but I don't think he will be very keen. He's already got one, you see."

King Arthur: "Well, uh ... Can we come up and have a look?"

Frenchman: "Of course not! You are English types."

— Monty Python and the Holy Grail (1975)

INTRODUCTION:
RE-EXAMINING THE ALPHA BET

Like the elusive holy grail, alpha is something everybody seeks, many claim to have, and few are willing to offer further explanation on.

How much alpha is out there for the masses of active managers? Any discussion of alpha hinges on the exact definition of alpha. Disentangling the returns to certain risk factors from those representing pure alpha is no easy task. Like the grail, everyone knows what alpha means, but no-one seems sure of how to identify it. For this section, we will use the following definition of alpha:

$$r_{i,t} = \alpha_i + \beta_i r_{m,t} + \varepsilon_{i,t}$$

Whereby the return on any asset i at time t may be explained by alpha (α), beta (β), and an error term (ε). In general, alpha will be equal to that part of excess returns not explained by the beta factors or any random errors. A further explanation of the distinction between alpha and beta follows below.

Alpha versus beta: a zero-sum versus a positive expected return game:

- Returns arising from exposure to systematic risk factors (β) are positively compensated in the long run, while alpha is a zero-sum game (or a negative sum game after fees).

- β is superior in reliability, predictability and cost to alpha, which is why *beta is in any case the cornerstone of investment returns.*

- Beta is about passive returns from taking on long-term risks that others don't want to bear. For example, a premium may be found for traditional beta such as domestic or foreign stocks, alternative beta such as emerging markets, or hedge fund beta such as small cap exposure. These are explained below.

- Alpha is uncorrelated with beta, whereas most betas have at least some correlation with each other. Alpha therefore provides powerful diversification benefits within an investment portfolio – hence its attraction.

Traditional beta funds deliver exposure to:

- broad equity markets
- broad bond markets.

Alternative beta funds offer exposure to the above, plus some additional betas such as those shown below, with the total risk usually distributed more equally:

- credit risk (high yield, emerging market debt)
- emerging market equities
- inflation-linked bonds
- commodities
- private markets.

Hedge fund beta funds require shorting, leverage and derivatives, *and* offer exposure to:

- style factors (for example, small cap versus large cap, value versus growth)

- event risk

- volatility

- risks of commercial hedgers in futures markets

- liquidity risk

- spread risk and carry trades.

When alpha transforms into beta

One might doubt whether any objective, systematic, rule-based approach to selecting assets can ever amount to true alpha rather than representing the bundling together of a set of some form of systematic risks. Even the subjective notion called "discipline" by fundamentalists could in fact be nothing more than yet another screening algorithm. Fundamental or "skill-based" managers will say their edge lies in experience, wisdom and their insights as to the specifics of individual stocks. "Systematic managers" allegedly exploit persistent market inefficiencies and do not even attempt to develop in-depth knowledge of the stocks in which they invest. The latter group has gained a substantial market share as investors demand structured investment processes. Our next interviewee comes from just such a firm.

Introducing Stan Beckers, PhD

Stan is Head of Alpha Management at Barclays Global Investors. Prior to joining BGI in June 2004, Stan worked for Barra for nearly 20 years, establishing and managing their non-US operations. He then became Global Head of Investments for WestLB Asset Management, and more recently was Chief Investment Officer of Kedge Capital, a wealth management organisation belonging to a Swiss family. His work has been widely published, and he remains a Visiting Professor of Finance at the University of Leuven in Belgium. He received a PhD in Finance from the University of California at Berkeley.

We will ask Stan to revisit some of the fundamental alpha concepts.

Stan, thanks for your time. First, can you define alpha for our readers? What are some of the common conceptions and misconceptions?

The most straightforward and intuitive explanation of alpha is skill-based returns that cannot be replicated by following a formula or some recipe or procedure. Skill can also be thought of as "divine inspiration". It's a finite commodity and, as in any skill-based game, the more highly skilled players gain at the expense of the lesser-skilled ones. Therefore, alpha is something you take away from the competition and nets out to zero. After fees it's a negative sum game. It's always difficult to disentangle alpha and beta because we have not uncovered all the betas yet. Arbitrage pricing theory, which succeeded and extended the capital asset pricing model, led to the discovery of additional beta factors such as small cap, dividend yield, or value versus growth. As the world evolves, we become more knowledgeable.

Could you comment on what you think separates good alpha from bad alpha (and beta)?

All alpha is good if we think of alpha as a pure skill-based source of value added. If the alpha is pure, it's good. If alpha has hidden beta in it, it's not going to be independent of broad market events, so it will not be as additive as originally thought. It will be contaminated, and somewhat difficult to deal with in portfolio construction.

You recently co-authored a paper called "Funds of hedge funds take the wrong risks".[1] In this paper you mention that investors should look for minimal common factor exposure. Could you expand a bit on that for our readers?

My basic premise is that people invest in hedge funds looking for alpha. Unfortunately, it turns out there are lots of betas embedded in the fund of fund returns. These are some of the more basic (or plain vanilla) betas as well, explaining 40% to 80% of fund of fund returns. So the hedge fund industry is far removed from being institutional quality, because people are not getting what it says on the label. Most hedge funds are not focused on delivering a pure

---

1 Beckers, S, Curds, R and S Weinberger, September 2006, "Funds of hedge funds take the wrong risks", *Investment Insights*, Barclays Global Investors.

alpha product, or any type of product that can justify their fees (on average).

Do you think it possible to actually quantify the total amount of alpha available across the industry?[2]

I think the short answer is no. The inefficiencies in the market are highly cyclical and will vary through time. If we think about alpha as what the skilled players take away from the unskilled, then the demand–supply imbalance between skilled and unskilled players is important. The industry as a whole is becoming ever more sophisticated and the nature and extent of the inefficiencies evolves continuously. So it's difficult to put a number on it. But we know that double-digit alphas are rare and usually unsustainable to the extent that people that are skilful will have difficulty in maintaining that edge (one possible exception being Renaissance[3]). Does the edge lie in being a quant (i.e. observing strict mathematical rules and formulas?) or in being a fundamentalist? They are probably the same, as at the heart of a good quant process will be a fundamental insight. Otherwise we revert to data mining.

What do you think of the single manager multi-strategy versus fund of funds debate? Can you compare and contrast them?

This is horses for courses. Multi-strategy has the advantages of fee netting (just charging one layer of fees). Based on that distinction alone, multi-strategy will have an advantage. But that presupposes that multi-strategy managers have a comparative advantage across a broad range of various strategies. This is rare. Most multi-strategy funds will have their generic roots in, for example, convertible

---

2   An interesting comment was made some time ago by Duke Professor David Hsieh when he suggested that the overall amount of alpha available in the hedge fund industry was only around US$30 billion. Subsequent commentators have suggested that he may not be far off since $30 billion represented about 3% of alpha on the then $1.1 trillion industry, and that a 3% "free lunch" sits quite well with many academics – J Willoughby, 27 March 2006, "Anyone here seen alpha?", *Barron's*.

3   Renaissance is a hedge fund, started by Jim Simons in 1982. It is considered in the industry to be the most consistently successful hedge fund, yielding returns 10 percentage points higher than legendary investors Bruce Kovner, George Soros, and Paul Tudor Jones. Because it is so successful, it charges a 5% management fee and a 44% incentive fee. Extremely secretive, for over two decades Renaissance has been at the forefront of research in mathematics and economic analysis. Renaissance trades with such high frequency that it at times accounts for over 10% of all the trades occurring on the Nasdaq.

arbitrage, and have branched out from there out of necessity. Convertible arbitrage returns are highly cyclical and dependent on emissions.[4] To maintain alpha they have bolted on equity, fixed interest or volatility trading without necessarily having advantages in them. Another possible disadvantage of multi-strategy funds is that they have single-manager (operational) risk. Funds of funds have the comparative advantages of potentially being more broadly diversified and being able to choose the best of the breed. I believe both can play a meaningful role assuming they play on their strengths.

Wherein lies the added value for fund of hedge funds?

To the extent that people want access to broad-based alpha, the funds of funds can do it for you. It's a pretty daunting task right now to find skilful alpha producers among the 8,000 to 9,000 funds out there, given that large subsets are mainly delivering beta rather than alpha returns. So, true fund of funds should be able to identify pure alpha. Plus they add their operational and legal due diligence.

Can you comment on the persistence of top quartile managers in hedge funds compared to the long-only world?

I do believe there is on average more skill in the hedge fund than in the long-only world. A skilful hedge fund player can do so much better in an unconstrained environment. (S)he should be able to deliver more value added in the long/short world, with fewer constraints and more flexibility. Hence, the higher persistence of top quartile hedge fund managers doesn't surprise me at all. I think it is very encouraging to observe.

Another interesting observation is that information ratios for hedge funds remain much higher than for long-only managers (for example, 1 to 2 versus 0.5 or lower). Do you believe that such figures are

---

4 This refers to the issuance of (in this case) convertible bonds. Some deem the convertible market as less interesting now given: a) the lower supply: low interest rates, high equity valuations and abundant profits have given less incentive to issue convertibles (one reason you add the call option is to lower your interest rate payments – but why would you do that if you can issue high yield at such low spreads); b) the increased demand from CB arbitrage funds has made the CB market more efficiently priced than before; and c) the environment (the extreme low volatility has reduced option prices).

representative of the industry? How much of the additional added value is absorbed in fees? How do you see trends in this area going forward?

The higher information ratio is just another reflection of higher skill and more persistence. As information ratio equals alpha divided by alpha volatility, a higher information ratio reflects a relatively lower volatility and therefore more persistence. An information ratio of 0.5 makes you a hero in the long-only world. In the hedge fund world anything above 1 does the same. If alpha on average is zero, then the information ratio is on average zero. The higher the information ratio, the more likely it is that competitors will try to emulate this comparative edge. It would surprise me if the high information ratios would eventually not be arbitraged away. However, the exponential growth in hedge funds doesn't seem to have had any material impact on the information ratios delivered by the industry so far.

Would it perhaps be because a lot of claimed alpha is actually persistent beta?

This could be the case. If you think about it, a Sharpe ratio for long-only funds may be 0.3 to 0.4. For a well-diversified portfolio of betas this can hit 0.7 to 0.8, so a long-term persistence of high information ratios may indeed point to the existence of hidden betas.

Two of your colleagues demonstrated that Information ratio = Information coefficient (ability to forecast) × √ (Breadth of opportunities).[5] Can you expand for our readers to what extent traditional and hedge funds can still improve on one or the other?

Well, the information coefficient measures skill. There is more skill in the hedge fund world. Why would you want to be a long-only manager as you can have more breadth and no constraints? So I have no problem with the claim that the hedge fund industry has acted as a magnet for the more skilful managers who have migrated from the long-only world. In addition, hedge fund managers have more breadth since they can take advantage of both over- and undervaluations and use a much broader range of instruments to implement their ideas.

---

5   Grinhold, RC, and RN Kahn, 1999, *Active Portfolio Management*, McGraw-Hill.

The number of ETFs has exploded, offering low-cost exposure to a wide range of markets and market segments. How do you see the industry of beta providers developing? What kind of new exotic beta strategies and ETFs will we see? Will investors be able to recreate their own hedge fund factor exposure using ETFs?

Absolutely. The proliferation in ETFs, which are becoming more exotic by the day, means that most conceivable risk premia can now be traded as ETFs. So, access to risk premia has now become cheap. The man in the street can buy into asset classes we didn't even know existed a couple of years ago. ETFs accelerate the restructuring of the industry into beta and alpha providers. ETFs support a real paradigm shift.

Can you comment on the hedge fund indexing tracking and cloning debate? Which one will be more popular going forward, or is there no place for either approach? What are some of the limitations of these techniques?

If we step back and observe that the hedge fund industry delivers lots of beta and little alpha then any index of the industry is virtually all beta. Clone providers have latched onto this and are packaging up the betas embedded in the hedge fund industry. To some degree they are selling the undesirable component of the industry. Nobody should actually buy such a combination, especially because they are not selling anything that most people don't already have exposure to anyway. Suddenly if you put "hedge fund replicator" on it, it achieves a magical attraction. I don't think that in its current form the hedge fund index clones have a meaningful role to play. There is however probably a market for "alternative beta", which is less easily traded.

I also think the whole factor stability debate amongst hedge fund replicators is academic. Obviously the mix of betas embedded in the hedge fund industry will vary through time. I would say that this is an accident rather than the result of clever engineering. It depends on the supply of dumb players, opportunities, etc. So chasing varying hedge fund factor exposure through time is not a meaningful process. We know from the long-only world that factor timing is a very low value added endeavour, and low breadth. So I do not hold out much hope for the hedge fund clones providing value added through factor timing either.

A recent report from Merrill Lynch (2006) suggests the hedge fund industry could probably plateau by 2011 at between 8,000 and 9,000 funds, pointing out that the growth trajectory for hedge funds is similar to that of US mutual funds in the 1980s and 1990s. What's your view on this? Oversimplification or reality check?

There's no magical number here. Obviously growth cannot persist indefinitely. However, if the segmentation of the business into separate alpha and beta suppliers is going to happen, then most active managers will gradually transition into pure alpha players (or hedge funds). If that evolution is going to take place, the number could go up into tens of thousands. Of course, the number doesn't matter as much as the size of the players.

Stan, you've worked with many different nationalities. Do you find many differences between the different cultures in terms of risk aversion/return expectations?

I find this a very intriguing question. Yes, there is a difference. What is it? Even if we think only about Europe, it is quite remarkable, in fact, that various nationalities have various comparative advantages in asset management. The French do well in cash management and short duration fixed interest, the British in equities. Does it relate to culture or engineering? It's difficult to answer. There are also inefficiencies based on culture: I would guess that, for example, there are more inefficiencies in Spain and Italy than in Germany or Holland. You can think of a similar argument when comparing Japan to the US.

What are some of the key lessons you picked up from spending 20 years at Barra?

That the world does not move nearly as quickly as we expect or one could rationally argue should happen. So the culture of risk management for instance is still glaringly absent in the hedge fund world. Lip service is being paid to quantitative risk measures. So it is surprising how hard it is to reconcile the innovative, creative element of asset management with the discipline of portfolio construction. They almost seem to be incompatible, except for the quant managers. It continues to amaze me how much value gets passed up in being cavalier about portfolio construction and risk management. At least the language of beta and risk factors is now becoming embedded in the industry. It is part of the institutionalisation of the business but the hedge fund world is still years behind the long world in terms of delivering an industrial strength, institutional-quality product.

What subjects do you still teach at Leuven University?

I teach investments and portfolio management once a week. There's benefit in having a foot in the academic world. It's a benefit to the industry too. It's a win–win situation. You never know if you understand something until you have to explain it.

How do you see the investment industry in 10 years time?

I foresee the industry segmentation that we talked about earlier. A huge ETF industry and a lot of assets for the hedge fund industry. But the industry needs to be more tightly regulated. The SEC (Securities and Exchange Commission), etc. have backed off so far. Obviously the industry doesn't want to be regulated. Regulators are surprisingly timid.

Finally – investment: art, science or skill?

It definitely has to be art and skill. Science is a tool to implement the skill in a more surgically clean fashion. Science as such doesn't bring any value added to the table. Scientists are certainly not above-average investors. Successful investing has nothing to do with IQ but everything with the creative processing of information in a way that most people don't. You need to do it differently and more quickly. You have to be individual and contrarian. Your premise as a portfolio manager has to be that you are right and everybody else is wrong. That explains why the industry is dominated by prima donnas.

Thank you for your time.

CONCLUSIONS

Although the initial hedge fund concept dates back to 1949, it has taken until now for sufficient data to become available to allow academic research to examine the underlying factors driving returns. Clearly alpha and beta are constantly being redefined as evolution continues. Significant academic and industry debate remains as to whether hedge funds should exist as an asset class in itself, or should be seen as pure alpha generators.

At present, the balance of opinion seems to conclude that we are heading towards a dual world with low-cost, passive beta providers on the one hand, and high-cost pure alpha providers on the other hand, and a world in which the emphasis will lie more and more on quantitative techniques.

In any case, for trustees the dual world will significantly alter their way of thinking, away from the traditional approach using divisions by asset class.

PART II: THE INVESTMENT ENVIRONMENT

3. A BRAVE NEW WORLD

An interview with Ben Inker
on the investment environment

"Economics is a science which studies human behaviour as a relationship between ends and scarce means which have alternative uses."
– Baron Lionel Charles Robbins (1898–1984)

THE LONG-TERM PERSPECTIVE

The end of the Goldilocks era has brought about a number of arguments for change to portfolios typically maintained in the past by traditional investors:

- 25 years of lower interest rates and inflation have led to massive capital gains in equities and bonds. Investors are at the moment faced with fair equity valuations, with most global markets trading at between 12 and 17× forward earnings.

- Investors are faced with an environment of low yields, where capital gains in especially bonds may perhaps be more limited.

- Equity managers have increasingly relied on best ideas, emerging markets and shorting, all of which is higher risk, while fixed-income managers have increased allocations to credit markets and sources of portable alpha.

- To reduce volatility in returns and increase downside protection, demand for less correlated products and private markets has increased.

On the one hand, a number of parallels may be observed to the late 1960s:

- Flat and periodically inverted yield curves worldwide have reduced opportunities for bond investors.

- A troubled US dollar and geopolitical tensions. The US is involved in a protracted war, straining fiscal resources.

- The emergence of new economic powers. From the late 1960s, Japan and Germany contributed much to global economic growth, while during recent years this role has been taken over by China and India.

- A key difference is the much greater presence of institutional money now, which may prevent the severe rise in interest rates and P/E contraction which occurred during the 1970s. We are however facing higher energy prices, which are this time demand driven, rather than supply constrained as was the case during the 1973 and 1979 oil shocks.

On the other hand, a number of alternative products have become available for both wholesale and retail investors that have potential to add value to the performance of a traditional investment portfolio.

Pension funding crises in certain countries and the lower return outlook are causing funds across the globe to rethink their investment strategies. The major themes resulting from this rethink are a reduction in listed equity allocations, a move to liability-driven investment approaches in some countries (often resulting in increased fixed-income allocations) and increased interest in a range of alternative assets.

Introducing Ben Inker

Ben Inker is the Chief Investment Officer at GMO, responsible for quantitative equities strategies in global developed markets and director of asset allocation. He is also a member of GMO's Executive Committee. Ben joined GMO in 1992 following the completion of his BA in Economics from Yale University. He is also a CFA charter-holder. GMO was founded in 1977 and remains a privately held global investment management firm servicing clients in the corporate, public and endowment and foundation market-places. The firm's approach is based on several key underpinnings, including discipline, a value orientation, investment research and constant innovation. We will discuss with Ben some of the more important recent economic and market developments, including the trend towards alternatives.

Ben, thanks for participating in this book. First of all, can you comment on "life after Greenspan" and the "brave new world" investors are facing?

There are so many ways to go with the "brave new world" idea, and it is astonishing how many of them fit today:

- *If you understand investing as taking on risk to achieve a return, there are more ways of separating out those risks than ever before*, giving the managers of investment pools unprecedented ability to pick out the risks they want, and avoid the ones they don't. This has helped to lead to a brave new world of diversification among institutional investors. Investors who stuck largely to domestic stocks and bonds 20 years ago now have allocations to international and emerging stocks and bonds, private equity, real assets, infrastructure, hedge funds of all stripes.

- *The old logic of a "prudent investor" investing as others do has been turned on its head* as investors race each other to be "cutting edge" – being the first to invest in a strategy or asset class.

- *But it is also a brave new world at the moment in that investors are generally feeling astonishingly brave* – the return they demand for taking a particular amount of risk seems lower than we've ever seen before.

- *As for life after Greenspan – for well or ill, we live in a world where central banks have much less power to control the financial markets than they once did.* Bernanke is probably as competent a Fed chief as Greenspan, which means he knows what to do in the event of a banking crisis, but unfortunately he has one basic tool, short-term interest rates, with which to achieve the Fed's simultaneous goal of permanently low inflation and high employment.

- *Today there are so many ways of funding investment that do not involve the banking system, and so many potential problems that low short-term rates cannot fix*, that Bernanke, or Trichet, or Fukui, may well be seen in the passage of time as failures against Greenspan's success because they simply cannot achieve all of the goals that are demanded of them with the very limited tools at their disposal.

Bernanke has been blamed for almost everything from a falling dollar to the housing bubble. How do you think he'll do and what are the main challenges he faces?

The biggest challenge Bernanke faces is that the two most dangerous features of the US financial system, *the housing bubble* and *inappropriately narrow risk spreads*, are not something he can "fix" through interest rate manipulation.

If US housing prices continue to fall, he will almost certainly lower interest rates, but the only way that helps is by reinflating the bubble, only to have it pop later. If houses get too expensive relative to incomes, they will come down, either by having house prices fall, or having them rise slower than incomes for an extended period of time. As we saw with the Japanese response to their stock market bubble in the 1980s, stretching things out over a longer period doesn't necessarily make them more pleasant. Unfortunately, in the end, the challenges that Bernanke faces are problems not particularly well adapted to his toolkit. He could easily get blamed for that, but it will make no more sense than giving Greenspan credit for the relative tranquillity of the 1990s economy in the US.

Where do you see the main risks to the financial system?

- *The biggest risk seems to us to be the profoundly interconnected nature of risk-taking,* coupled with inappropriately narrow risk premia. Many players seem to have forgotten that bad things can happen. Who knows where the next crisis will come from – US housing, European high-yield debt, a currency crisis, a major terrorist attack, a failing hedge fund? The strength of the current financial system is that there are so many players who have been willing to take on risks, and that is simultaneously its weakness.

- *Once upon a time, credit risk was the preserve of banks.* In a crisis, authorities stepped in to recapitalise the banks to keep the system going, and banks being banks, credit risk was their business, and they would then start to lend again. Today, credit is being extended by all sorts of actors. Banks, hedge funds, CDO investors, insurers, etc. All of that demand has helped push down credit spreads to some of the narrowest levels on record, but most of these players are not "in the business" of extending credit. They are in the business of trying to make money, and if they begin to see credit extension as riskier, and/or less lucrative than they had believed, they may try to exit en masse.

- *Even if the initiating trigger is something else entirely – a currency crisis that causes hedge funds to lose big on their carry trades, for example – the waves across the financial markets could be devastating,* as investors taking solace in the "liquidity" of their positions attempt to sell them and find no willing buyers. The big difference between the LTCM crisis and a potential crisis today is that LTCM took generally good bets, but was inadequately capitalised, while the system today is taking a lot of bad bets, but is well capitalised. The LTCM event didn't have much long-term effect, because very little money was actually lost. Investors in LTCM lost some, but the investment banks who took on the positions made it all back pretty quickly. This time, a lot of money will be lost, and the implications will be long term.

We have reprinted below a 7-year forecast from GMO.[1]

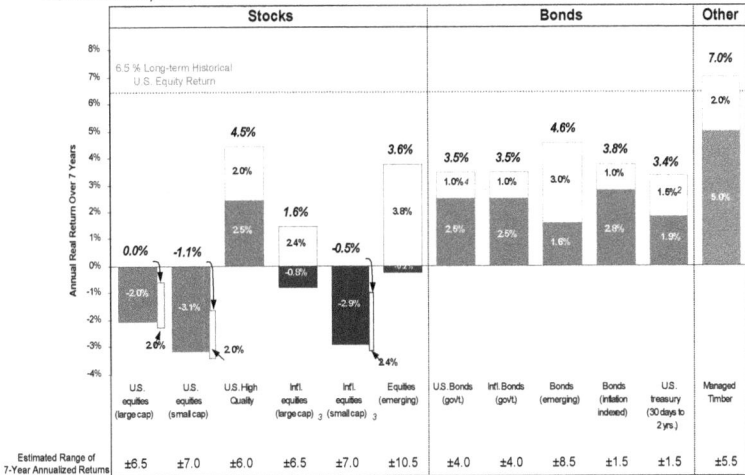

GMO 7-Year Asset Class Return Forecasts*

As of June 30, 2007

Courtesy: GMO

---

1   GMO, June 2007.

Ben, can we query why you use 7-year numbers? I'm sure people have asked you that before. Is there academic evidence that it represents the average mean reversion time?

There is no magic to the seven years. The basic assumption is that at the end of seven years, everything will be trading at fair value. If we used five years or ten, for example, it wouldn't change the rank ordering of assets in any meaningful way, so in one sense it isn't all that important a choice. But the reason why we use seven years is that it is the historical average reversion time for equities, and if you don't know anything special about timing, which we don't, the safest assumption is that it will take an average amount of time to revert to fair value.

Can you comment on the asset classes you like in the new environment (especially alternatives)?

I wish I could! The most striking thing about today's environment is that practically every risky asset looks overpriced.

- *There have been other times in history when the headline equity indices have been more overvalued – 2000 is an obvious example – but we cannot find any previous time in history that such a broad swath of assets is simultaneously expensive.* At current levels we believe all of the major sectors of the global equity markets are overpriced, credit spreads are universally too narrow, yield curves give too little premium for duration risk.

- *The pricing pressure in alternatives is looking extreme.* Cap rates in the classic alternative of real estate have in many cases fallen below the yield on the debt they support, which is a sign to us that they are infected by the same valuation trouble as stocks. Private equity deals are getting done at higher and higher valuations, with more and more debt, which hardly seems hopeful for the prospective returns there, and the weight of money coming down the pike does not suggest things will get better soon.

- *Even timber, one of our favourite alternative asset classes for the basic reason that it was generally unaffected by prior asset class pricing cycles, has been affected.* Ten or twelve years ago, you could buy forest land in some places for less than the value of the trees standing on it – the implicit land value was actually negative. Today, internal rates of return on timber properties have fallen into the 4% to 5% range, with many buyers simply using timberland as a vehicle to speculate on land price appreciation driven by suburban sprawl. While it is possible that the speculators will be right, they certainly aren't going to get rich off of the income spun out by their trees, since they are paying far too much.

- *Oil and gas, infrastructure – the very fact that you merely need to mention starting a fund in these areas to be greeted with a flood of interest (and money) suggests that they are unlikely to be havens either.*

- *And that leaves us liking the most unlovable asset class of all, cash.* Unfortunately, cash seems to be the one asset that a sophisticated institutional investor cannot own, but in a world where risky assets offer little or no premium for the risk they embody, cash is an obvious alternative if you could just use it.

- *Barring that, we do like high-quality stocks within equities.* High-quality stocks – stable, profitable companies with low debt – have been left behind in the rally of the past four years, because they did not generate the kind of spectacular earnings growth of more cyclical and volatile firms. High-quality stocks usually trade at a premium to the market, but today they are actually cheaper than the market on many measures, and will probably provide a significant amount of downside protection if something should go badly wrong. Unfortunately, they are not cheap enough, in the US or elsewhere, to make a lot of money in absolute terms, but they are one of the few asset classes we believe will beat cash over the next seven years.

What's your outlook for inflation and what type of real assets do you expect to keep generating real returns during periods of high inflation?[2]

Our official outlook for inflation is benign – 2.5% in the US, and similar in most of the rest of the developed world. Call us wide-

---

2 Extensive academic and professional literature provides ample evidence that traditional asset classes such as stocks and bonds have not provided adequate inflation-hedging capabilities in the past, but have in fact generated returns with a negative correlation with inflation.

eyed optimists, but we believe measurable inflation will even creep back into Japan in the coming years. There is a risk of inflation getting out of control, though, since monetary policy is still pretty accommodative around the world and there isn't a lot of spare capacity to be had.

If inflation should spike up, it unfortunately isn't clear what assets will hold up well.

- *Commodity futures* are no panacea, since inflation need not be driven by commodity prices and the markets are anyway pricing in a significantly negative roll yield.

- *Real estate and equities* are trading at high valuations, held up by cheap and easy credit, so if higher inflation leads to higher rates, they will be unlikely to help.

- *Timber* has historically provided excellent diversification in such times, but it has never started at today's valuation.

- *Short duration inflation-indexed bonds* are pretty much guaranteed to do well in a high inflation environment, but they won't make a lot of money in real terms, just continue to tick away.

- *Cash*, again, looks like a nice haven, since yields will rise quickly if inflation fears return.

Do you see a role for commodities in a balanced portfolio, from a beta (long only) and/or alpha (for example, CTA, spread trade) perspective?

- *We are quite worried about the prospective returns to "commodity beta".* While there has historically been a return to being long commodity futures, commodity futures are not at heart a financial asset. Financial assets give returns to investors. That is, after all, their reason for existing. They transfer money between those who have capital and those who need capital, and as the capital goes in one direction, income and capital gains move in the other. Commodity futures are different. There is no inherent reason why there needs to be a return to being long commodity futures, any more than there is to being short commodity futures. If there has been such a return historically, it is our belief that it stems from the old Keynes argument that the true hedgers in the commodity markets are generally producers, and therefore net short to guarantee a price for their output. Commodity production is generally a capital-intensive enterprise, and it would therefore make sense for commodity producers to lock in a price for their output, even if they had to pay something of an insurance premium to do so. In the old days when the hedgers and speculators were the only players in these markets, the hedgers could "bribe" the speculators to take the other side of their trades by building in a "roll yield" to the pricing of the futures markets. Today, there is another set of players, who are price-insensitive long-only investors in commodities. These days they are large compared to the true hedgers, and we do not think it is a coincidence that the roll yield from being long commodities is at its most negative in history. The imbalance in these markets seems to be on the long side, and if there is a return to commodity futures today, it may very well be to being short, not long.

- *As for CTAs*, the commodity futures markets are inefficient, just like most other markets. It should be possible to find investors who are good at finding these inefficiencies. But finding those investors is a skill in itself. Anyone who feels they are good at uncovering investment talent should certainly look at CTAs as well as other active management strategies, such as hedge funds. But it is unclear whether CTAs as a group will add much value (it is certain that active equity investors as a group don't, by comparison) so a decision to invest with CTAs is at some level a vote of confidence in your own ability to find above-average managers.

Does gold have any use in investors' portfolios (considering that it does not have much economic value and costs money to store)?

We don't understand gold. Most commodities are all about flow. A commodity is produced and used, and the standard laws of supply and demand determine the amount produced and the price of the commodity. Gold is different:

- There is a huge supply sitting in vaults around the world, so even if we stopped mining it, it isn't as if we'd "run out" any time soon.

- Its price is generally higher than seems warranted by its industrial and ornamental use.

- People view gold as a store of value, and have for a very long time. They may indeed continue to do so into the indefinite future. If so, it will probably be a good store of value, particularly in inflationary times. But given that it doesn't provide any income, the best guess we can come up with for the expected return to gold is the inflation rate. And if that is all you are going to get from it, you'd be better off with inflation-indexed bonds.

Perhaps we are missing something, but to me, gold seems more like a vehicle for *speculation* than an *investment*.

Ben, from your 7-year forecasts, you prefer US bonds to US stocks. Can you expand on that? I'd guess most people now prefer cash plus products given the flat yield curves? Wouldn't the risk in the bond market now be on the downside?

We do think the risk in the bond market is probably on the downside, and we generally prefer cash-like and cash plus investments to bonds.

- At the moment, US investors are paid more to be in cash than in bonds, and since real bond yields are fairly low, we don't believe there will be any capital gain on the bonds to make up for that. But we do expect cash yields to fall over the next few years and expect the yield curve to be positively sloped on average over the next seven years. Right now, we favour cash over bonds, but as the yield curve steepens in the coming years, we expect to change that view.

- On the topic of stocks versus bonds and cash, we like stocks less than either. The reason is a simple one, although not quite as simple as it was in 2000. Price/earnings ratios on most stock markets are modestly above long-term averages, which itself would suggest sub-normal returns to stocks. But we believe that the P/Es are flattered by current profit margins, which are at an all-time record high. Never before in history have corporations made as large a fraction of global GDP, or had such a high aggregate return on equity, and we do not believe that these good times will last. If profit margins were to fall towards normal levels, stocks will be revealed as substantially overpriced. Our favourite measure of value is price to cyclically adjusted earnings, popularised by Robert Shiller, and on that measure, almost all stock markets around the world today are quite substantially above historical valuations. If they revert to normal over the next seven years, stocks will be very hard pressed to keep up with either bonds or cash.

In terms of the quality cycle, you are extremely bullish on high-quality stocks. Can you elaborate on that?

One of the most striking features of the global economy today is the extraordinarily high level of corporate profits. Over the course of four years, we have seen the sharpest increase in aggregate profitability in history. The biggest beneficiaries of this burst have been those companies which have either high operational leverage (that is, cyclical and/or capital intensive companies) or high financial leverage. Not only have these companies seen their earnings grow hugely, but they have been re-rated by the markets as if they are permanent growth stocks.

Our definition of quality includes, as two of its main factors, stability of profit margins and low leverage. These companies therefore are the ones least likely to have benefited from the rising tide. High-quality companies are more profitable than they have been on average, but the margin by which that is the case is much smaller than for many other stocks. In a sense, it is therefore not a surprise that they have gotten left behind in the rally in the markets since 2003. Since they have been so comparatively dull, today they trade at a discount to the stock market on many measures, whereas for most of history they have traded at a substantial premium. If we are right that today's profit margins are not sustainable, we believe that high-quality stocks will outperform handsomely. Not only will their earnings hold up better than the average company's, but they will probably move again to a premium valuation relative to the market. We do not expect their returns to be immensely high in absolute terms, but relative to other equities, we believe they are both lower risk and cheap, which is a combination we love.

What do your "value versus growth" indicators point to at the moment?

We are believers in value. That means that in our view *valuation is the primary driver* of what assets will do well and do poorly in the future. There is no such thing as a high return asset class – only an asset class which is generally priced to deliver a high return. Value stocks, as traditionally defined, are usually priced to beat the market. While they always trade at a discount to the market – that is, after all, how "value" is defined – in most of history that discount has been bigger than could be justified by their worse-than-average prospects for future profits and profit growth. Today, however, the discount that value stocks trade at is much narrower than normal, and we believe that they are actually priced to under-perform growth stocks. This imbalance is most pronounced in the US, where our forecast for value stocks is 3.4% per year worse than growth over the next seven years, but in the EAFE (Europe, Africa and the Far East) markets we still believe that growth should beat value by about 0.5% per year for the next seven.

Almost every manager we meet up with, whether they classify themselves as thematic top-down or quantitative bottom-up, is underweight the US and overweight Asia and emerging markets. How much longer will this be a justified bet? What catalysts are needed for a further re-rating?

It's always worrying when the rest of the world agrees with your investment judgement. One of our primary fears about our current underweight to the US and overweight to Asia and emerging is that the consensus is seldom right for long.

• The case for the overweight and underweight is straight-forward. The US is the most expensive large market in the world, and most of Asia and emerging are significantly cheaper. You don't have to have a particularly rosy view of the prospects for China or Asia generally in order to want to be in markets where they are cheaper. Adding in the fact that a number of these currencies are cheap and likely to appreciate versus the US dollar over the next seven years, and it is a case that more or less makes itself.

- The biggest risk to this basic idea is that governance, both corporate and macroeconomic, has not improved as much in these countries as seems to be the case. We have always believed that emerging market stocks were riskier than developed market stocks and therefore we wanted to get "bribed" to own them, in the form of a higher expected return. The only way we know how to get a higher expected return out of an asset is to have it trade cheap, so we have contented ourselves with buying emerging stocks when they trade at a discount to developed, and not otherwise. Today they look comparatively less risky than they used to. The economies appear to be managed better. The companies seem to be managed with some concern for the desires of outside shareholders. They look, with some notable exceptions, much more like normal companies that happen to be domiciled in emerging markets. If that is all sustainably true, then the discount they need to trade at can shrink, leading to a further upward re-rating. If it is an illusion fostered by the generally benign environment, valuations will need to fall.

What do you think of the narrow spreads in emerging market debt at present? Are they supported by economic fundamentals?

We actually rather heartily dislike the asset class of emerging debt. With the current low spreads (author's note: around 200 basis points at the time of the interview), there seems to us very little additional good news to be had in the asset class, and we know what the best conceivable outcome for them is – about 1.6% better than US treasuries. The downside is considerable. While economically most emerging countries are in good shape, and they appear broadly willing to pay their debts, there is no guarantee this is a permanent condition, and we'd rather see wider spreads to compensate for the risk of things changing. Our forecast for the asset class is for it to actually underperform US treasuries. The only positive thing we have to say about the asset class at all is that it is an inefficient one, and our bond team has managed to consistently add several percentage points a year over the benchmark. It is hard not to like that alpha potential, but the asset class looks like a losing bet.

What's your view on less liquid alternatives such as private equity and infrastructure?

We aren't experts on either private equity or infrastructure.

- In the case of private equity (when did it stop being called leveraged buyouts?) we have a hard enough time finding two sources that agree on what the historical returns have been. But even if historical returns have been good, we can't help but be worried about any asset class or strategy that has been flooded with money. Private equity is a game of finding a presumably undervalued company, taking it private, "improving" management, and then taking it public again a few years later. Since for the most part the owners of the company when it was public were institutional investors, the limited partners in the private equity funds are institutional investors, and the buyers of the IPO when it eventually comes will be institutional investors, the only thing that is assured about the round trip is that the private equity firms and investment banks will make a lot of money along the way. It's far less clear or certain that the institutions will have benefited, but if the private equity firms have some secret knowledge about how to run companies that ordinary managers are not privy to, or at least aren't interested in using when at public companies, then capital might at least be more efficiently used.

- One thing is certain about illiquid assets. The best performing pools do far better than the worst, so the scope for active management to add value seems larger than in traditional asset classes. For any investor who considers themselves particularly skilled at finding above average managers, private equity can therefore make a lot of sense. But it is much less clear to us that there will be particularly good returns to the average dollar invested.

- In infrastructure, it is clear that the IRRs on the deals have been dropping in recent years as interest in the asset class balloons. At best this means returns will be lower than in history. At worst, it means this is an investing fad, abetted by easy credit conditions, and pricing will weaken considerably in future years.

What new research projects is the team working on?

We think we know a lot about reversion to the mean. What has always been a mystery to us is the timing. What causes some bubbles and busts to go on longer and farther than others? Can we find some way to avoid the class value manager's fate of being too early to buy and too early to sell? Improving our ability to time the shift in a market from greed to fear and back again would be a real help. At some level, the turning points are inherently uncertain, but if we can gain better understanding of the probabilities at any given time, it will be a big help.

Are there any important developments in the quantitative space worth noting?

It's hard to speak of the "quantitative space" as if quantitative managers do things in a similar way. One trend for quantitative managers that is in place has been going on for a long time – as computing power and data availability increase, there is a temptation to try to use all of that power and data, which means higher frequency modelling and more turnover. We haven't gone that route in our equity or asset allocation portfolios, but someone clearly has, to judge by what is happening to turnover levels in all sorts of markets.

How do you see the investment industry evolving over the coming decade?

Ten years ago, we would have said that a decade from now indexing would be a much larger portion of the market, and investors would look to active managers to provide alpha in a fairly pure way.

With the benefit of hindsight, we can say that the world did move in that direction, but with much less speed than we thought.

Ten years from now, we would expect the same trends to continue. If we are correct and the next ten years are also characterised by generally low, and fairly similar, returns across asset classes, we may see something of a shift among institutions to look more to finding managers they believe have alpha and concern themselves less with what asset class they happen to invest in to achieve that alpha.

Finally – investing: art, science or skill?

All of the above. *Investing has aspects of art*, in that there is not, and will never be, a set of equations that allow you to consistently outperform – even if such equations could be found, their very use would change the landscape so that they ceased to work. Imagination and creativity will always be required to outperform, even for quantitative investors.

Investing has aspects of science in that quantitative modelling can be a huge help, in testing your ideas, in building efficient portfolios, and keeping your emotions from destroying the power of your insights.

And investing is a learned skill, in that there are lessons that must be experienced to really understand. An investor who hasn't lived through a serious bear market simply does not know what risk truly is. A quantitative manager who hasn't over-engineered a portfolio and lived through the consequences can't simply be "taught" the virtue of simplicity in modelling, or the importance of understanding what the insights you believe you are capturing really are. Of course, experience doesn't always help – in a serious bull market, the best performing managers will almost certainly be young and overconfident, since prudence and humility are not easy to square with the big, risky bets that will pay off the most.

Investing is not a science like physics where laws last forever. *In investing, what you can hope to understand is what mistakes are being made and how long they will last.* You should not be overconfident when you find behavioural finance anomalies such as small caps or value. Many times, inefficiencies are set due to the way people are paid; that is, there is a lot of career risk at stake which is due to the agency problem. Although incentive fees and co-investing may help a bit, I haven't figured out the perfect structure for incentives yet.

Thank you for your time.

CONCLUSIONS

Ben is a firm believer in mean reversion and the view that asset class returns are predictable in the long term. As usual, the difficulty lies in figuring out the timing of the reversion. Delivering attractive absolute returns in the long term remains the key issue, although there's always the relative risk of shorter term results being too different from clients' expectations for a balanced portfolio. The picture that Ben paints of the "brave new world" is a bit bleaker than we expected. In some ways, it makes sense as risk is priced at a historical low, and also, no matter how often risk gets sliced up and redistributed, somebody will be left holding the hot potato. Ben's emphasis on the limited ability of the central banks to intervene during future periods of systemic crisis is also worth pondering, and as such the risk of moral hazard may have increased to a point beyond what most investors bargained for.

When queried further, Ben mentions his favourite invest- ment ideas are on the short side; for example, British pension fund demand has pushed down real yields on UK 50-year infla- tion-linked bonds to a level he finds hard to believe (author's note: around 75 basis points at the time of the interview).

Although some alternatives we discussed with Ben may offer low correlated returns and better downside protection than traditional assets, investors need to be aware that the flip-side to higher alpha- adding opportunities may involve lower liquidity and transparency and an increase in fees. And as Ben points out, especially within the alternatives space, manager selection becomes crucial.

PART III:
EMERGING MARKETS
– BOOM OR BUST?

4. THE ROAD LESS TRAVELLED

An interview with Dr Mark Mobius
on emerging markets

"I've toured rubber plantations in Thailand and road-tested bikes over the pothole-ridden roads of rural China. I've choked on roasted camel's meat, sheep's eyeball, guinea pig and dined (surprisingly well) on scorpions on toast, all to find undervalued companies before other investors do. I think you could safely say that I'm driven."
– Mark Mobius, in *Passport to Profits*

INTRODUCTION

Emerging markets continue to fascinate investors, and whatever they do, they always promise an exciting ride.[1] In this chapter we discuss some of the fundamental changes in emerging markets. At a broad level, the pros and cons of investing in emerging markets have long been widely acknowledged. The arguments *in favour* of exposure to these markets include:

- They reside in economies which are seen as dynamic, have achieved stronger economic growth than more developed economies, and look set to continue to do so.

- The markets and economies are seen as having enormous latent potential. China alone is expected to represent 20% of world GDP by the year 2020, becoming the third-largest

---

1 Several definitions of "emerging market" exist, including the IFC's based on per capita GDP and MSCI. The MSCI Emerging Markets index contains some very developed high-income countries such as Taiwan and Korea, where access by foreigners remains limited.

economy in the world. And 85% of the world's population lives in emerging markets, 60% in Asia ex-Japan. Population ageing in these markets is projected to be a much smaller drain on future growth than it will be in much of the developed world, especially Europe and Japan.

- In many of these countries, the emergence of a professional and consumption-orientated middle-class is driving a strong pick-up in domestic demand. At the same time, an enormous pool of cheap labour combined with often artificially controlled, undervalued currencies means that these countries are super-competitive against developed economies in manufacturing and, increasingly, in services.

- These markets normally trade at a discount to developed markets, suggesting that investors are not required to pay up for the greater growth potential. Naturally, the discount reflects the higher risk of the sector (especially in terms of corporate governance).

- Scope for added value from active management is greater due to the lower proportion of institutional ownership and less efficient dissemination of information.

The major *negatives* include:

- Volatility is high for a range of reasons, including the narrow economic bases of the underlying economies plus the various crises, including political and currency crises, which have afflicted the sector on a reasonably regular basis. Volatility is increased by the tendency for contagion across markets; that is, when a crisis develops in a particular emerging or Asian market, it frequently spreads to other emerging markets including those where there is no logical link with the original crisis.

- Transaction costs are higher and liquidity lower than in developed markets. The lower liquidity itself leads to volatility as the markets have difficulty in absorbing the positive or negative cashflows which occur when they move into and out of favour with institutional investors.

- Standards of investor protection trail those of the more developed markets. Issues under this general heading encompass broad legal systems, corporations law, stock exchange regulation, including information disclosure and corporate governance, as well as repatriation laws.

Introducing Dr Mark Mobius

Mark has spent more than thirty years working in Asia and other parts of the emerging markets world. He currently directs the analysts based in Templeton's eleven emerging markets offices and manages the emerging markets portfolios. Mark joined the Templeton organisation in 1987 as President of the Templeton Emerging Markets Fund in Hong Kong. He has served on the World Bank's Global Corporate Governance Forum as a member of the Private Sector Advisory Group and as co-chair of the Investor Responsibility Taskforce.

Mark holds bachelor's and master's degrees from Boston University, and also earned a PhD in economics and political science from MIT. Mark has studied at the University of Wisconsin, University of New Mexico, and Kyoto University in Japan. Mark is the author of several books, including *The Investor's Guide to Emerging Markets, Equities, Mobius on Emerging Markets, Passport to Profits* and *Mutual Funds.*

Given his extensive travel experience, as he spends most of his time jetting around the globe looking for the gems in exotic countries, some investors have nicknamed him the "Indiana Jones of investing".

Mark, what are some of the major economic and financial trends at the moment in emerging markets?

1) *Economic growth*: Emerging markets are growing much faster than the developed countries in North America, Western Europe, Japan, Australia and New Zealand. The emerging markets combined average annual growth was 5.5% over the 10-year period ended 2005, which is more than double the 2.7% growth recorded by the developed countries during the same period. Economists expect this growth trend to continue for the foreseeable future.

2) *Inflation*: Inflation has been on a downward trend in emerging markets, supporting a high growth environment. The rate of increase in consumer prices has nearly halved to 5.4% pa in 2005, from the double-digit numbers seen in 1998–99. The IMF forecasts inflation to be stable in 2006 and fall further to 4.8% pa in 2007.

3) *The interest rate spread on emerging markets bonds* has fallen significantly in the past five years from more than 1000 points to less than 200 basis points (less than 2%) at the time of this interview due to rising liquidity and low inflation.

4) *Net direct investment* inflows into emerging markets are expected to reach a record high level of US$211 billion in 2007 following US$185 billion in 2006. Key drivers included strong economic growth, robust corporate earnings, favourable financing conditions and stock market appreciation.

5) *Portfolio fund flows* into emerging markets totalled US$24.6 billion in 2006, the highest in the past ten years and nearly 50% more than the US$16.9 billion in 2005.

6) *Stock market performances*: emerging markets have recorded substantial price appreciation in the past few years. In fact, of the 26 countries in the MSCI Emerging Markets index, 18 of them reached record levels in 2006 or 2007.

Let's talk a bit about corporate governance in emerging markets. In the old days, a lot of especially the smaller listed companies used to be known as ATMs for their majority (family) shareholders. How much has changed? Are many of these countries and companies still "family first, foreigners second?" When will the discount to developed markets disappear?

Over the years I have seen significant improvements in the standards of corporate governance practiced in emerging markets.

In general, we feel that family-run businesses in emerging markets have come a long way. The Asian financial crisis brought the need for changes to the forefront and pushed companies to reform. Even countries with significant family-owned companies, such as South Korea, have brought their practices more in line with international markets. For example, recently the Finance Minister announced that anti-takeover or other defensive measures would not be introduced in the corporate sector despite calls from local entities.

A discount in the valuations of emerging market companies is not necessarily linked to the fact that these companies are at a higher risk of abuse from family shareholders or management. After all, take a look at US companies such as Enron or Worldcom – what happened there? (Mark also notes that the European Union at times has prohibited shareholders from exercising their rights as shareholders in influencing management.)

The discount to developed markets could disappear when investors are convinced that emerging markets companies are not necessarily riskier than developed markets companies.

What should investors be aware (wary) of when investing in emerging markets?

Investors should be prepared to invest for the long term. Stock prices are not only dependent on fundamentals but also on market sentiment. A change in either can cause stock prices to experience great volatility, be it in emerging markets or in developed markets. Investors should also be aware of the different types of risks (economic, liquidity, operational and currency) involved in investing in emerging markets so that they are in a better position to make an informed decision. Of course, the above cautions are not different from investing in any market, emerging or developed. It is just that emerging markets on an individual basis can be influenced by more dramatic changes.

What emerging country would you never invest in?

Never say never; I don't intentionally avoid any market. All countries are potentially an investment target.

Some investors are wondering whether they should invest across the full range of emerging markets or in Asia specifically. Do you have any preference for one approach or the other? Perhaps you can contrast the main differences in composition; for example, commodity versus non-commodity exporting economies.

We are finding bargains across all emerging markets including Asia, thus the preference really depends on an individual's risk profile. While Asia is the largest emerging market region in the world, a portfolio with exposure to global emerging markets could result in a lower risk profile via means of greater diversification.

In general, investors seem to prefer regionally diversi-fied funds over dedicated country funds as they provide the broader opportunity set. But we note lately a lot more interest in dedicated country funds (for example, China/India or a number of available BRIC – Brazil, Russia, India, China – products). What do you think about that? A lot of country funds were closed after the last Asian crisis in 1998. Is this a sign of another bubble? Do you think investors should invest in country funds?

I think it's a sign of an emergence of a class of more sophisti-cated investors who are not afraid of incurring higher risk levels in exchange for higher returns rather than a sign of another bubble.

Moreover, in addition to Asian markets, many other emerging markets have learned lessons from the Asian crisis. Countries have improved their foreign reserves and balance of payments posi-tions dramatically, lowering their vulnerability to external shocks. Additionally, the implementation of financial, structural, social and economic reforms has benefited their economies. As such, markets are in a much stronger position today.

Investing in a country fund could give investors the required diversification and in fact reduce risk if it forms part of a larger investment portfolio. Bottom line, investing in country funds would really be dependent on an individual's risk profile.

Do you have any comments on the recent volatility in China?

"A" shares have had an extraordinary run, making them more vul-nerable to declines and volatility. In fact, Shenzhen "A" shares are trading at a P/E of 74×, while their Shanghai counterparts have a P/E of 34×, both significantly higher than Hong Kong's P/E of 14×.

In a bull market that has run for nearly four years with little interruption (the last major fall in emerging markets was seen in May–June 2006), corrections such as these can be expected. In retrospect, after the decline in May 2006, markets rebounded and reached new highs.

Our long-term view on China remains positive. Average GDP growth rate in the past four years was 10.3%. Despite the Chinese government's efforts to slow it down, it is still expected to be one of the fastest growing economies in the world. The country continues to take great strides towards becoming a major global player, thanks to strong government policies that support investment.

What do you think would be the best way to play the China story? Hong Kong listed shares, Greater China funds, ETFs, or other?

For the novice investor, ETFs or Greater China funds could be considered. Greater China funds may be the better option though, since they allow investors to benefit from not only the developments in the region but also from the vast experience and knowledge of the fund manager. For more experienced investors, they may want to make their own investment decisions; in this case, investing in the Hong Kong listed "H" and "red-chip" shares could be a possibility. However, this could be more risky as his or her investments may not be as diversified as in an investment fund which has exposure to many stocks.

What do you think of the Chinese property markets?

Currently, property markets in second-tier and third-tier cities are relatively healthy. Demand is mainly from end-users and property prices are affordable. But in first-tier cities such as Beijing and Shanghai, I would say that there may be bubbles. Property speculators and investors have driven up prices to an unsustainable level. Thus, as the recently implemented cooling measures take hold, there may be a correction. However, in the long term, property prices should continue to increase, but at a more gradual pace. In general, rising incomes and higher living standards should lead to greater demand for housing in China. Increasing land prices will also have an impact.

**Is China spending too much money on non-productive
fixed asset investments, especially given the huge
appetite for cement and steel?**

China's economy has been driven by two key areas – exports and
investment. However, with China now growing at its fastest in a
decade, over-investment in selective industries of the economy has
raised cause for concern. Positively though, the government has
recognised this and has been implementing measures – which have
been having some success – to curb the over-investment in sectors
such as cement and steel.

**How far behind in years is India versus China in terms
of infrastructure development? Can you comment on
the pros and cons of a centrally guided economy versus
a free market economy in an emerging market context?**

India is probably about 15 to 20 years behind China, which is
expected considering India's economic liberalisation started about
20 years after China.

Emerging markets would best benefit from a mixed economy.
While a free market economy promotes characteristics such as pro-
ductivity, innovation and efficiency, a centrally guided economy theo-
retically has more social advantages to control finances and resources
to ensure the provision of public goods, social welfare, and so forth.
Unfortunately the implementation of centrally planned programs
has been riddled with inefficiency, rigidity and corruption.

Take the cases of India and China. A key difference between
the two countries is the relatively more centralised and authoritative
Chinese government which enables it to make decisions and utilise
resources with little opposition, while India's democratic structure
results in slower decision-making and implementation.

While the Indian government lacks the centralised planning
implementation as possibly seen in China, India's democracy, albeit
a cumbersome one, could work to its advantage in the longer term.
If government controls on privatisation for example are eased in
India, the democratic background will enable the country's private
sector to benefit since decisions will be based on free market forces
as opposed to government choices. In reverse, China's rapid growth
has led to overcapacity in many sectors as investment decisions
were not based on a free market economy.

What interesting countries do you think will enter the MSCI Emerging Markets in the coming years and how can people take advantage of that beforehand?

A number of African countries, Croatia, Vietnam and Middle Eastern countries such as Saudi Arabia, Bahrain and Oman are some countries that come to mind. Investors can gain exposure to these markets by investing in mutual funds that already have investments in these countries.

In general, we find that managers generate higher excess performance in emerging markets because these markets are less efficient. How long do you think it will stay that way? I note the language and cultural barriers.

With greater globalisation and the entry of more and more investors into emerging markets, market efficiency is only getting better. Yes, there are language and cultural barriers but those can be easily overcome by working with local people like we do at Templeton. My investment team is spread across 13 countries globally. However, despite this, chances are that some level of market inefficiency will always remain. After all, look at developed markets – inefficiencies exist there too. To generate higher returns, managers must study the fundamentals of the company, market and sector that they are investing in to ensure that they can make an investment decision to the best of their abilities.

Any favoured countries or industries for the longer term?

While we have been finding good companies in many countries, we believe that markets such as South Korea, China ("H" and "Red-chip" shares), Taiwan, South Africa, Brazil, Turkey and Russia present excellent investment opportunities. South Korean and Taiwanese companies offer a good combination of good technological and production expertise. South Africa has excellent companies at attractive prices. China stands to benefit from its accession into the World Trade Organization, greater foreign interest and strong consumer spending. Brazil is a country rich in natural resources and benefits from the continued high prices of commodities such as iron ore and pulp, which are the country's major exports. The key to Russia's economic and financial recovery has been high oil and other commodity prices resulting in a build up of strong foreign reserves which will subsequently lead to higher corporate earnings. Moreover, we continue to believe that Turkey's substantial progress on the implementation of structural reforms, support from the International Monetary Fund and continued efforts to ensure European Union accession should make Turkey an attractive investment destination.

For some time, we have been emphasising four major themes in our emerging market investments that we call the "four C's". These are: Consumer, Commodities, Convergence and Corporate Governance. Sectors that are geared towards direct consumption will continue to benefit from the higher disposable income per capita in emerging markets. With commodity prices at relatively high levels, there will be many opportunities for good profits for companies supplying them. Convergence in regions such as Asia between China and the rest of the countries or Eastern Europe's convergence with the European Union will continue to provide good opportunities for companies. Finally, corporate governance is very important in investing. We want to invest in companies that treat investors fairly.

Do emerging markets still offer value? Emerging markets seem to have done extremely well on the back of the commodity boom which has benefited countries such as Russia, Brazil and South Africa. What kind of long-term returns can investors expect going forward?

Yes, definitely. Market fundamentals support the long-term uptrend of emerging markets. While emerging market companies have recorded significant price appreciation, corporate earnings have also increased, making valuations still attractive. The opportunities are plentiful. Many companies are experiencing strong growth and there are many upcoming IPOs in many emerging markets. The key is to find undervalued companies that are well capitalised and have a unique and competitive product range. Companies that are paying solid and sustainable dividends are especially attractive. Despite their rapid growth, many emerging markets companies are undervalued when compared to their peers in developed markets. We target long-term average annual returns of 15%.

With the increase in correlation with the developed markets (especially during stress periods), are emerging markets still an effective portfolio diversifier?

Yes, as long as the correlation between emerging markets and developed markets is less than 1. The correlation between the US and emerging markets for the 10-year period ended 2005 is about 0.7. There is a good chance that the correlation between emerging markets and developed markets could widen as domestic investors become more important than foreign investors who are currently dominated by US investors.

Some firms that also run value-style investments in developed markets do not visit companies, and do very well. Do you think the improving data quality in emerging markets could justify such an approach as well at some stage?

Improving data quality would definitely be beneficial but I personally feel that numbers cannot replace the vast range of information one can grasp when on the ground. This direct first-hand approach provides the benefit of a timely understanding (both of the opportunities as well as the pitfalls) of the emerging market stocks we cover. Even things like a management's refusal to meet investors could ring a warning bell. This understanding and information cannot be gained via remote control from behind a nice big desk in places like London or New York reviewing second-hand reports. The fund manager has to make the effort to go out to these emerging markets and investigate for himself.

You used to work with the legendary Sir John Templeton. What are the key lessons you've learned from him?

Yes, Sir John Templeton demonstrated early on through his investing that developing countries were neither places to be feared nor avoided, but quite to the contrary could prove fertile ground for profitable portfolio investing, if done correctly.

The following are some of the key lessons from Sir John Templeton:

1) Buy value.

2) Buy low.

3) There's no free lunch.

4) Diversify.

5) Learn from your mistakes.

6) Don't panic.

What do you think of the increasing number of hedge funds entering the emerging markets space?

We think hedge funds are a positive influence. First, their fees are higher than normal investment management fees so that they have shown investors that good investment management must be paid for, and good returns puts the debate about fees on the back burner. Second, hedge funds have increased the degree of liquidity and volatility. For the value investor volatility is a good thing since it gives an opportunity to purchase stocks at below their intrinsic value and sell above their intrinsic value.

I read in one of your books that you used to teach technical analysis in Hong Kong. Can you comment on the use – and abuse – of technical analysis?

Technical analysis can be an effective tool to evaluate the execution price of buy/sell decisions since by definition the analysis looks to help predict future movements by studying the stock's price and volume history. However, some investors may use technical analysis as a short-cut to fundamental analysis, which involves an in-depth study of stocks. While this may work for short-term investors such as day traders, this is not a good idea for long-term investors since charts do not tell you anything about the fundamentals of a company. The optimal solution would be to use technical analysis in tandem with fundamental analysis. This would enable the investor to study price movements as well as assess the true worth of a company.

What do you think makes a good fund manager? You once quoted integrity, flexibility, insight, courage and long hours. In general, what do you look for when hiring new candidates?

First we look for discipline, humility, love of study and the willingness to work hard. Discipline is necessary to take a long-term view and to be patient. It is required to stand tough when all those around you are losing their cool. Then you must be humble and be ready to admit your mistakes so you are capable of changing. In addition to the attributes mentioned above, we look for people who can work well as a member of our team, as the team approach is part of our culture.

My final question – investing in emerging markets in the future: art, science or skill?

A combination of all three. Art is necessary to be creative. Science is necessary to examine the facts and interpret them objectively. Skill is necessary to understand the correct time to buy and the correct time to sell.

Thank you for your time.

CONCLUSIONS

The world of emerging markets remains exciting, although globalisation and developments in communication imply that we are all becoming increasingly integrated and in the long run the current inefficiencies and valuation discounts may disappear.

Emerging markets account for a number of the major economic trends of the last decade. They have provided the majority of additional energy and steel demand, reduced the rate of global inflation through their cheap goods and services exports, and, with liberalisation of capital accounts, represent a significant portion of new demand for international securities. In addition, their buying of international securities is no longer just US treasuries. As business activity continues to shift to low-cost countries, total global output may increase, though it may imply job losses in some of the developed countries.

Some international investors make a few trips a year to emerging countries in search of new ideas. Mark is a class apart; he spends over 200 days a year shuttling back and forth in his corporate Learjet between exotic locales.

Although emerging markets are not deemed as exotic and lawless as they once were, they will always attract a certain amount of apprehension, given the inherent market volatility. Investors might do well to remember the words of Mark's mentor, Sir John Templeton:

> *"Sure the world is full of problems. In all my years there's never been a year free of problems — big problems, and I never knew how they'd all be solved. In fact, some of them are never solved. You just learn to live with them."*

5. THE EAST WEST PENDULUM

An interview with Robert Lloyd George on the
shifting balance between East and West

"The pendulum of history which swung so visibly and decisively towards the West in the past 200 years is now beginning to return at an accelerating pace towards a twenty-first century world dominated by the East, in wealth, population, technology and economic dynamism."
– Robert Lloyd George in *The East West Pendulum Revisited*

INTRODUCTION

This chapter focuses on Asia as seen through its historical development; that is, the long-term perspective. As an introduction, we examine below two of the countries that make up only a small portion of global market capitalisation. Yet, there are important considerations in terms of the sustainability of their continued economic growth and the implications for the world economy.

China: An economic snapshot

- China runs a "hybrid" economic system – a mix of socialism and capitalism.

- Since the move to a market economy in 1978 the Chinese economy has quadrupled in size. GDP has grown at an average annual rate of 9%, while its share in world trade has risen from 1% to 7%.

- Measured on a purchasing power parity basis, China now ranks as the second-largest economy after the US.

- Growth has been especially strong in the coastal provinces near Hong Kong, Taiwan and Shanghai.

- The production base is moving from large state-owned enterprises to more nimble private companies.

- The recent accession to the WTO helps maintain strong economic growth rates, though tariffs had already been lowered substantially prior to China's membership.

What is China's impact on the global economy?

- *Asian currencies*: China's exports now contribute 7% of global goods exports. The strength in exports puts upward pressure on the renminbi. Should China further revalue the renminbi, it is likely that other Asian currencies will appreciate.

- *Commodity prices*: China now accounts for the bulk of commodity demand, which has pushed up prices and depleted inventories. Resource prices are underpinned by China's economic strength and fewer new discoveries, as well as consolidation within the industry.

- *Global interest rates*: Cheap imports from China help reduce the rate of inflation, thereby keeping a ceiling on nominal interest rates.

- *Global output*: A relocation of business activity to low-cost countries will raise total global output but it will imply job losses for some other countries.

- *Global capital flows*: The Chinese government has announced that it will diversify the investment of its current reserves beyond sovereign bonds. Chinese firms may also increasingly seek to invest capital abroad as the capital account liberalises, thereby underpinning global capital markets.

India: What are some of the differentiating features from China?

- *Technology skills*: India ranks number one in the world in terms of foreign technology licensing, and second in terms of availability of scientists and engineers.

- *Language skills*: India possesses the second-largest English-speaking population in the world.

- *Growth drivers*: India's growth is consumption-driven (64% of GDP versus 43% for China), while China's growth has been investment-driven (45% of GDP). Historically India spent less than 4% of GDP on infrastructure (compared to 11% for China), though the government is now implementing policy measures to increase spending.

India: What are some of the similarities with China?

- *A history of reforms*: Whereas China started its open-door policy in 1978, in India reforms were triggered by the two-stage devaluation of the rupee in 1991. Similar to China, India started opening up its economy to foreign investment.

- *Increasing dependence on energy imports*: Both economies are becoming more dependent on external energy sources for their continued strong growth. In the third quarter of 2005 India slipped into a current account deficit of 2% of GDP, while China still remains in a surplus.

Introducing Robert Lloyd George

Robert Lloyd George is Chairman and CEO at Lloyd George Management. He was educated at Eton and Oxford University and began his investment career in London in 1974. After spells in the Paris Stock Exchange and banking in Brazil, he joined the Fiduciary Trust Company of New York to work on international investments for the UN Pension Fund. Robert was Managing Director of Indosuez Asia Investment Services in Hong Kong from 1984, before founding Lloyd George Management in 1991. He has published five books, including *A Guide to Asian Stock Markets* (1989), *The East West Pendulum* (1992) and *The East West Pendulum Revisited* (2005).

In this interview, we will ask Robert about some of the insights offered in his books. Robert will explain why he feels Asia is replacing the United States as the locomotive of the world economy and will recapture its position as the world's largest economy, a place it relinquished in the early 1800s with an event marked by the British Ambassador's visit to the then Chinese emperor Qian Long.

Robert will examine recent developments in the capital markets in the Asia-Pacific region and discuss economic growth prospects and opportunities for the longer term.

Robert, there is a great deal of interest in Asia at the moment. You published your first book on it in 1989, not long after the launch of the MSCI Far East index. How has your view on Asia evolved over the years?

I actually came to Asia in 1981, so I have been involved in the region for 26 years now. Initially I specialised in Japan, then gradually expanded into Korea and Taiwan, whereby I established some of the first country funds. In 1992 I focused on China and India as I thought these were the most under-researched markets with the most potential. Never would I have imagined the size of the markets today. Back in 1992, it was the macroeconomic fundamentals that improved and caught my attention. Nowadays it's the capital markets that have caught up with the fundamentals. Compare the landmark US$22bn listing of Industrial and Commercial Bank of China (ICBC) in October 2006, demonstrating investors' faith in these once infant markets. Seen in that light, I don't think the recent volatility in March is more than a healthy correction.

You estimate that by 2020, Europe, North America and Asia will be similar in terms of economic size. Could you expand on your main arguments for that for our readers?

The main arguments underpinning my forecast are:

- *Growth of free trade within Asia.* Especially China with Southeast Asia, India with the rest of Asia through Singapore, etc. We are seeing rising trade and capital flows within Asia rather than a reliance on US exports.

- *Demographics.* India and Vietnam have a very much larger under-30 population with rising consumer expenditure.

- *Global leadership and education.* For instance, Tata Consultancy Services (TCS) hires 12,000 software engineers every year in order to meet 40% growth in software demand.[1]

- *Financial evolution is at an early stage.* Mortgage lending and consumer banking is only just now coming up in many of the developing Asian countries.

---

1 As of 2006, TCS is Asia's largest IT services firm with revenues of over US$4 billion. TCS was featured in the book *Outsourcing to India: The Offshore Advantage* by Mark Kobayashi-Hillary. It topped the list of top 10 best performing IT Services providers worldwide for 2006, as rated by the IT business publication *Global Services*.

- *Political stability.* Compare Asia to other emerging markets such as the Middle East, and you will find that Asia presents a picture of stability.

In one of your books you mentioned that "the leadership of Asia, in economic and cultural terms, is passing to the Chinese". Can you comment on that?

It was in 1991 that I made that prediction. Part of it had to do with Japan being in a period of deflation and turning inward. It did take some time for China and the Southeast Asian countries to become a major source of demand. I believe that we're somehow recreating the Ching dynasty's tributary system where foreign countries and businesses (such as Korea, Vietnam, Thailand, Burma and some Western countries now) are sending emissaries to China to pay tribute and do business again with the "Middle Kingdom".

What's your view on the renminbi?

The renminbi has already strengthened from 8.3 to 7.8 to the USD now. If allowed to free float, I predict it could go to 5 to the USD. My sense is that perhaps there will be an acceleration of about 5% to 10% appreciation a year. One should respect the Chinese desire to go slowly. China doesn't want to be the subject of foreign speculation, so it's a rational response as capital markets open up.

What key drivers in history, culture, and religious beliefs make Asia still different from the West? Will we ever converge? What can Westerners learn from Eastern philosophy? Does it offer any help when investing in Asia?

- I'd say the most important drivers are the *work ethic* and *education*, which stems from culture. There is nowhere in the world where education is so emphasised as in China. Every single one of my staff in Hong Kong is taking an extra degree. There is a tremendous desire for self-improvement. For example, following the Confucian tradition, Taiwan has the highest per capita density of PhDs. The Chinese believe that if only a single boy in the family can attain a better life, the whole family will benefit.

- Another thing I'd deem important is the *high savings rate* combined with the lack of a welfare state. Compare this to, for example, Europe, where German students can take up to 10 years to complete their degrees and then live on handouts provided by the government. In contrast, in China there is a lot of emphasis on self-reliance and determining your own future.

Fundamental R&D and innovation are critical for economic growth, competitiveness and welfare. Asia has often been accused of lacking in innovation, and rather relying on implementation of ideas borrowed from the West. Outsource production to China and services to India. Do you think this is fair, and will this change going forward?

It is misleading and unfair to say that the Chinese are not innovative. China was a leader in navigation, hydraulics, medicine and a number of sciences for many centuries. In the 1980s Japan promised a lot (especially in biotech), but maybe the Chinese, who are a lot more unconstrained, may succeed better in innovation.

The US has always played an important role in Asia's history, ever since Commodore Perry's arrival in Japan in 1853. What role do you see for the US going forward?

The US has made a very important contribution, as a benevolent superpower. Now, the US is progressively downsizing its forces in Japan and Korea. (They are considering increasing their presence in Guam.) Perhaps the reduction in military might could reduce economic and political power too.

What could happen in the vacuum that would be created is that there could be a clash between China and Japan over, for example, Okinawa, the Ryukyus and oil and gas reserves. The Chinese naval build-up even has the Indians somewhat concerned.

What are the main potential internal and external shocks to the Asian system? For example, be they military, political, environmental or technological?

It will not be an internal shock (barring Kim Jong Il of course). I don't see any political worries. Probably it would be something like oil prices, or a global financial crisis (for example the US credit cycle – author's note, Robert was quite prescient on this as this interview was taken on the eve of the subprime crisis), a major global bank collapse, or an earthquake. I don't think Asian political or economic risk is very high. For example, two years ago people worried about the big four Chinese banks, but these have since been re-capitalised and successfully listed.

Are Indian Equities still an attractive asset class? Everybody seems to be saying they're overvalued. What could be the trigger for a correction?

I just came back from India, and I'm very optimistic. There was a 30% correction in June 2006, but the 30% to 40% corporate earnings growth is very strong and the market has since come back. Real estate in Bombay doubled in price last year. The budget was very positive and the government is pro-reform.

What are some of the hurdles India still faces in its development? (For example, infrastructure, political.)

India is still 10 to 15 years behind China, though there are lots of reforms and construction in railways and airports. But still, I'd say India is one of the big winners in globalisation; for example, look at Reliance, or ICICI bank. I'd say it is very important for the rural economy to be included in organised retailing and online banking.

What are your thoughts on Japan, as Japan still acts as a major destination for the exports of East and South Asian countries?

Japan remains undervalued, in my opinion. Small caps were hit following the Livedoor scandal in January 2006 (and underperformed for the rest of the year). In my opinion, the yen can strengthen. There is a new mood, with rising salaries and property values. I would not write off Japan as quickly as most people do. Look at the innovation over there. For example, Toyota is clearly beating Ford and GM, and look at its development in hybrid cars.

Apart from equities, what other alternative Asian investments would you consider worthy of investing; for example, REITs, hedge funds, antiques or other?

- *REITs* are very interesting. In Singapore, Hong Kong and Japan they offer very good yields. In many countries it remains very difficult to buy property directly, so I like the alternative they offer.

- As for *hedge funds*, I believe that in Asia you want to be long, as it is very difficult to time the markets. With the high fees in hedge funds, I would think interest in this asset class may peak soon.

- As for *antiques*, I love antiques. Two of my friends started "Chinese heritage funds". At the moment, in China over 1,000 museums are funded by the state, which wants to buy back heritage pieces from overseas. I'd say Sung dynasty ceramics are the place to be.

Robert, you have been managing Asian equities since the early 1980s. Has much changed in your investment style since?

Yes. Instead of using a telescope, we're now using a microscope. In the old days it was very much about buying countries, whilst nowadays we're using teams on the ground to examine micro and small-cap companies and scrutinise them using intensive analysis. One has to very much go under the radar and find the market inefficiencies and mispricing.

What are the main differences you note between American, European and Asian investors when it comes to investing in Asia?

Asia was deemed very exotic before; now there is much greater knowledge, appreciation and sophistication amongst investors. The British and the Dutch seem to be ahead of the pack, although many British seem to think Asian fund management can be done from London. The US are very ahead of the curve, while the Germans and French are miles behind. To US investors, Asia offers a very interesting alternative to an otherwise expensively valued domestic market.

What are some of the more interesting countries and sectors in Asia to invest in at the moment and why?

Vietnam is very small, but interesting. New frontier markets always excite me, such as Pakistan. China's global impact on resources will benefit other emerging markets such as South Africa and Ghana. Within Asia, we always like small caps (less than US$1bn in size), especially in Hong Kong and Singapore, although you'd have to be careful when liquidity dries up. It's similar to venture capital investing, whereby you have to take a five-year view.

If you invest in Asia, what can investors expect in terms of Alpha and Beta?

On a 20-year view, 12% to 15% would be reasonable to expect, including the down years. I don't believe a purely quantitative approach works very well in Asia. Indexing, for example, is very backward-looking. Take for example Malaysia, where market cap weights reduced from 23% to 5% and then 0% (when Mahathir closed the market to foreigners in 1998). Or Japan where the global market cap weight went from 40% to 10%. I remember Indonesia in 1988, where the market cap went from US$1bn to US$20bn in a year as capital markets became more reflective of the underlying wealth in the economy. How does one model that?

I prefer to go around the world looking for mispricing instead, such as when the Chinese economy grew by 10% a year for five years in 2000–05 and the Shanghai index declined by 50%. That gets my attention.

Apart from writing books, what else keeps you occupied?[2]

I have nine children, who keep me very occupied. Also, I have my business to run. Apart from that I like to collect books and antiques. As you pointed out, I very much enjoy writing. I play tennis and golf too.

Finally – investing in Asia in the future: art, skill or science?

I think you need both art and science. I've always believed that knowing Asian culture and history is vital, as well as having the same interests as the locals. For example, follow the activities of the big Hong Kong property developers (who are very astute and shrewd operators) for a while. I would consider it an art, in that a sense of timing is important, but also a science, in terms of good security analysis.

Thank you for your time.

---

2 Robert recently authored a book called *David & Winston* (2006), describing the friendship between his great-grandfather David Lloyd George and Winston Churchill during Churchill's formative years between 1904 and 1914.

CONCLUSIONS

According to the United Nations, over the next five years the global workforce is expected to increase by 7%. The developed markets of the US, Europe and Japan will account for only 3% of the additional workforce, while China and India are likely to account for 37%. Hence, there is likely to be a disproportionate amount of global output generated by these two countries. There is ample historical evidence of periods of economic integration resulting in multi-decade periods of high structural growth. Examples of these include Japan (1955) and the Asian newly industrialised countries (1967). Some of these countries were in the 1960s at similar wealth levels as the African countries, which since then have largely stagnated. Key differences include the focus on savings and education, as well as the build up of infrastructure that maximised the use of the abundant cheap labour and undervalued currencies. The Asian export model is useful, though an over-reliance on foreign demand and investment can make countries vulnerable at times. China and India can continue to achieve above average and more balanced growth rates, provided that the following requirements are met:

- ongoing reforms (especially in the financial sector)
- continued migration of labour from agriculture to the manufacturing/services sector
- efficient technology transfer
- improve income disparity and the middle class
- broadening of the capital markets
- improved corporate transparency.

The primary effect on the global economy of the sustained high growth has so far been felt mainly through rising commodity prices during recent years. Nevertheless, we believe that some of the structural changes, such as the disproportionate increase in the global workforce, are creating a profound secondary effect on the global economy as both countries continue to move up the value added chain.

PART IV: OPPORTUNITIES IN FIXED INTEREST

6. HIGH YIELD OR HIGH GRADE?

An interview with Jae Park on the use of
high yield and structured products

"Short debt makes long friends."
– Old English proverb

INTRODUCTION

One could argue that now is one of the worst times to invest in debt, with default rates rising from historical lows, and although spreads have recently widened, interest rates may still be considered historically low. It would seem that investors are rewarded with none of the upside but may face all of the downside when investing in fixed interest. Flat yield curves in a majority of the developed countries – downward-sloping even in some markets – make investors increasingly favour short-duration instruments and cash-related benchmarks.

In some cases, investors are expanding their opportunity set and looking at adding value through opportunistic managers who can use a combination of credit and alpha transfer to invest in any global credit market. Demand for higher yielding products has resulted in an increase in the number of exotic markets (beta) and arbitrage opportunities (alpha), many of which have now been added to the portfolios of investors.[1]

Apart from fixed income being substituted by low-volatility alternatives with a yield component (such as property, infrastructure

---

1 Exotic beta with a fixed income character includes: US syndicated loans, US preferred shares, high yield emerging market debt, ABS/MBS, global convertibles and CDOs. Exotic alpha opportunities refer to convertible bond arbitrage, fixed income long short, the distressed debt space and alpha transfer from other asset classes.

and certain hedge funds) by an increasing number of endowments and pension funds, the fixed-interest space is finding itself in evolution as managers move towards unconstrained benchmarks, and competition increases with low volatility (fund of) hedge funds.

Why do investors like to invest in debt?

- *Safe haven:* If equity markets go down in crisis situations, there is the traditional flight to quality to government bonds.

- *Stage of life:* Investors closer to or in retirement may prefer debt for income reasons or for the extra stability.

- *Tax advantages:* For example, municipal bonds in the US enjoy tax benefits. Similarly, in Australia some higher yielding segments (such as hybrid securities) come with tax credits.

- *Liability matching:* Some defined benefit plans use bonds to match the duration of their assets and liabilities.

- *Low absolute volatility:* Bonds in general have an annual standard deviation of 2% to 5%.[2]

In this chapter, we examine the risks involved in fixed interest and discuss the alpha and beta arguments for fixed interest.

Introducing Jae Park

Jae is Chief Investment Officer, Fixed Income at Loomis Sayles, a subsidiary of IXIS Asset Management. Jae joined Loomis Sayles in 2002 after more than 21 years with IBM where he served as Director of Fixed Income investments, responsible for the management and performance of the fixed income and cash assets for the IBM Retirement Fund. Additionally, he oversaw the strategy and implementation for non-US funds invested in local fixed-income markets as well as global fixed income hedged to different currencies. Jae also served as Head of Fixed Income investment research and as a portfolio manager while at IBM. He is a graduate of Cornell University and earned his MBA from Columbia University.

---

2   Note that low bond volatility is becoming less of an argument for investing in this asset class as institutional investors can achieve this by leveraging/de-leveraging other instruments. However, investors are then possibly taking on factor exposure (for example, to equity markets).

We talk to Jae about the debt cycle in different asset classes. How can investors use alternative fixed-interest markets to improve their overall yield while managing risk? We also examine the likelihood of a worst-case scenario and the expected loss for fixed-interest investors.

Jae, thanks for your time. First of all, are investors likely to meet their targets in general bond funds given the current environment, or will we see a downward revision of alpha and beta targets?

Meeting performance targets from a risk-adjusted relative return (alpha) point of view will require a keen sense of awareness of current and future investment opportunities. This is actually nothing new for excellent fixed-income managers. Over time, we have seen markets evolve, become more global, and to capture these opportunities, guidelines have been revised to allow more ways to generate alpha.

What this does is allow the truly excellent to excel, but it also has the potential to create mediocre performance from others by delivering a steady diet of higher risk beta.

New opportunities are always emerging and the ability to go short will play a role in meeting performance targets. You need to become more efficient in recognising value. *So it is my expectation that we can meet alpha targets but there will be a need to continually innovate,* look far and look near, exploit all levels of volatility, and develop methods to capture the opportunities. We'll need to capture risk premiums at more bond-specific levels, opportunistically, and prepare to capture broader beta opportunistically as cycles play out.

While it is generally considered harder to predict beta, *I don't see further downward revisions for beta; these revisions have already been made in recent years.* The last four years in the US, the Lehman Brothers Aggregate Index returned just under 4% annualised and most allocators use current yield less defaults as a proxy for future returns. The math will take care of a good portion of it.

What are the prospects and challenges for global fixed-income markets?

You've already identified many of the challenges.[3] Clearly, while we have general stability, and it may continue for a while, we face a future that is sure to be unstable and to include a cleansing process that is uncertain in magnitude. Going forward, I tend to be an optimist, in that I expect many global fixed-income opportunities to present themselves, including currencies, country and sectors. I could be considered a pessimist in that I expect human (greed) factors to drive markets to extremes and then develop cracks. *In the meantime, taking risk within specific opportunities while being generally defensive appears the prudent strategy this late in the cycle.*

Are investors mispricing risk?

While mispricing is a term used in an arbitrage sense, I will use it here to describe pricing that does not reflect "true fundamentals". Is there a disconnect between fundamentals and asset prices? There is often more than one way to price a security as investors have different needs and time horizons as well as risk tolerances. They each drive a unique pricing function, so mispriced for one investor may not be so far off for another. Nothing is really cheap, except maybe the yen, but don't fight the technicals. Timing has always differentiated the outstanding investor from the pack.

While fundamentals can change, the frameworks for risk premium pricing do not change dramatically, nor often. Most of the time, market pricing reflects the fundamental information available but it is influenced by supply demand dynamics. The traditional risk premiums demanded by traditional investors have been overshadowed by engineered product demand as well as the cycle that has been much discussed – the financing of US assets from overseas investors driving down US yields. In a more perfect, "transformed" world, you drive the premiums down and reach a steady state of equilibrium. That assumes that engineers have figured out a way to reduce risk in risky assets and that demand continues indefinitely as a result of global prosperity and balance. It will unwind and risk

---

3 Jae refers to our earlier comments on the general low level of interest rates, risk premiums and leverage in the system.

will be priced more appropriately, but short of a massive disturbance or recession, we can expect cheapness to be short lived.[4]

Where will the next credit event likely come from and how much are investors likely to lose?[5]

This is hard to say without a crystal ball. It seems to me anytime there are new instruments and strategies that have not been through a full cycle, it's a good place to look. Defaults and devaluations flushing through the system are always the other areas to be wary of. Steep yield curves have created problems in the past (savings and loan, mortgage derivatives) and the US real estate market certainly was impacted by it recently with the adjustable rate option payment mortgages and other product innovations. The yield curve inversion is currently having an impact on lower credit mortgages but could become more of a contagion if there is further deterioration in real estate prices accompanied by an economic slowdown.

In the early nineties, it was the junk bonds and leveraged buyouts. From 1992 to 1994 it was the mortgage derivatives and Mexico, followed by the Asian crisis in 1997 and Long Term Capital in 1998. In 2001 we had the popping of the tech bubble.

I expected to see more fraud and rogue trading in hedge funds – we've seen some come along with Amaranth. We saw some early signs of correlation trading challenges with CDO hedging in the credit default swap market when Delphi hit. I can't help but expect the combination of leveraged structures utilising CDS, perhaps in the leverage loan area, will be the next major credit event. (Author's note: this interview was conducted a few months before the subprime crisis hit.)

What do you think of the emergence of unconstrained credit opportunities funds?

This makes a lot of sense. Of course you have to do everything correctly, and have a good fundamental process. It is very difficult to

---

4   Jae implies here that due to the demand, short of a massive disturbance happening, the current low yield environment is likely to persist.

5   Credit event: a specific event (most likely credit default) that could upset the global financial system.

run a credit-only mandate against the Lehman Corporate index. If, say, you focus purely on security selection you may be forced to take bigger bets than you originally intended to. Releasing constraints on duration, etc. will help a lot.

How can investors best use high yield and structured credit within their portfolios?

You tend to get paid for a variety of fixed-income risks in the long run, just don't make a large allocation at the tightest spreads and at the lowest default levels in a cycle.

In opportunistic portfolios, be truly value-driven by doing solid research, don't overpay and don't be overly exposed to names that can widen with a downturn in the economy that drives higher defaults. Wait patiently for good valuations. Make sure you have solid fundamental research coupled with smart quantitative tools.

What is your opinion on the trend towards illiquid markets (for example, private debt)?

Again, it comes down to doing good credit analysis, because if things turn sour, you will get hurt much harder. I do have a problem with very illiquid structures. In general though, private debt has been around for a long time, especially with insurance companies, and is worth considering. Private mortgages are a great niche market.[6]

Let's talk a bit about emerging market debt. Are the current spreads realistic?

Yes, given the low default probability out there it's actually very realistic. High energy prices, upgrades in credit ratings, currencies that should get stronger and not devalue − all the signs point to a realistic spread level. I'd argue it was too wide in the past so EM debt was always a good buy if you could stand the volatility. It was my favorite asset class for the longest time because you could make so much money in it. We are now investing in local EM debt.

---

6   There are a few firms that made investments in capabilities to originate and invest in private mortgages backed by niche commercial real estate. These may include NYC co-ops, shopping malls, etc. that have solid assets backing the loans with excellent terms. These are not to be confused with private sub-prime loans.

In general, do you think currency should be treated as an alpha source for international fixed-income portfolios or does it depend on the specific market involved?

International fixed-interest portfolios may be part of a larger currency overlay program. The allocation to alpha in currencies is well accepted, although it is also accepted that your currency manager may underperform for three to five years. Fundamental drivers need to be in sync with short-term trend following and diversification. Even within our fixed-income portfolios, we may wait for technical confirmation of fundamentals. I firmly believe in currency alpha, but as always there are plenty of mediocre managers that go out of business or currency scams chasing retail markets.

What do you consider some of the more interesting alternative debt markets from a beta perspective (for example, syndicated loans markets)?

I think bank loans are indeed interesting, so are high yield and emerging market debt. The compensation for default risk has been high on average.

What developments do you see in the credit derivatives markets? How will they affect fixed-income strategies?

It will eventually evolve to the point where cash managers like us can effectively utilise them but client documentation will remain a challenge. More sophisticated long/short strategies and thinking will develop over time. We are hiring specialists to get us there sooner.

What do you think of the increasing convergence between fixed-interest funds and low volatility hedge funds?

This is a necessity of the times. I note that Fixed Interest managers may actually have different alpha correlations. We recently hired a Director of Alpha strategies, to extract alpha from our sector and product teams, and start a multi-strategy fund. We're also adding several alpha sleeves such as from long short credit, arbitrage, TIPS versus nominal, etc.

Fund of hedge funds or single manager multi-strategy?

Based on personal observations, I'd say there are some very successful single manager multi-strategy managers out there. I think that's the model for the future. There is more transparency too. With the recent hedge fund explosion, it's hard to believe there won't be a fall out, as we haven't been through the full cycle yet. Stay with established managers, and avoid the rogue traders. Funds of hedge funds need to maintain a very high level of due diligence.

Is the trend towards benchmark unaware absolute-return fixed-interest investing (that is, cash plus products) genuine and is it gaining momentum?

Anyone who understands what alpha is can port it to any benchmark in theory but less so in practice. Cash or cash plus is just another benchmark. Many products in the hedge fund space have a lot of embedded beta as opposed to beta timing so we need to see if the next generation of products coming out are more beta neutral. It appears to be gaining momentum but I wouldn't say it is mainstream by any means.

Can you comment for our readers on how alpha transfer has been successfully used in the fixed-interest space?

The most successful alpha transfer strategies tend to use derivatives to access markets and hedge beta risk. Others use cash strategies and hedge out the beta risk. One of the first alpha transfer strategies was actually a "short duration cash" strategy[7] which is not as effective in an inverted short end environment

---

7   For example, a cash strategy that invests in short maturity bonds, floating rate bonds, asset backs, plays duration bets on the short end along with rolling down the yield curve all with a duration less than 1 may more consistently beat Libor by 100 to 150 basis points than a traditional equity manager can beat the S&P by 100 basis points, given for example a 2% tracking error. In the simplest sense of alpha transfer, you overlay S&P 500 futures on to the cash and transfer "cash strategy alpha" to the equity markets. Given that part of this strategy takes into account the very steep short end of the curve, when it inverts the strategy loses one of its structural advantages.

but very good most of the time. This strategy effectively beat Libor and, by overlaying S&P futures on it, transferred the cash alpha to the equity asset class. Others involve global fixed-income mandates accessing bond and currency markets, along with managed futures in equities and commodities. With the development of CDS, long short credit is a reality. We have developed multi-strategy fixed-income products that utilise global alpha, long short credit alpha, government alpha as well as hedged bank loans. *This reflects my conviction that alpha is nothing new but is simply about clearly identifying the drivers of perform-ance.* The technology has been around for nearly two decades – multi-factor risk models that have isolated or decomposed returns into factors. By hedging away systematic factors you are left with alpha.

Can you compare bond alpha versus other alpha pools in terms of quality and sustainability?

I've always been a big fan of bond alpha versus other sources of alpha in terms of quality. If you have a true understanding of bonds and bond sectors then you can see why some fixed-income firms have dominated with more consistent performance than in any other asset class. Because bond prices are dependent on cash flows and the certainty of those cash flows, fixed income lends itself to quantification better than other asset classes. Granted that there are uncertainties associated with default probability, structural complexities and option analysis but the type of analysis required differs from predicting a P/E multiple expansion and contraction or the price dependencies based on growth prospects. Then there is the compounding aspect of yield that compensates for the risk over time. This compounding dominates all fixed-income sector returns. Price fluctuations even out over time but provide opportunities for alpha with good timing.

Value investing works in fixed income when frameworks are carefully developed and investor insight is captured effectively. I used to say during the dot-com bubble there is no such thing as growth bonds but I guess that didn't prevent a lot of investors from buying telecom bonds that went to zero and were never going to benefit from any meaningful upside.

When dealing with fixed-income alpha (for example, arbitrage strategies) how should investors deal with the negative skewness, high kurtosis and fat tails?[8]

I have a very simple way of looking at it. Did you actually lose the money through a default? That's a very fat tail that is not acceptable. In '98, anything that was not a treasury on-the-run lost money relative to that sort of security. The degree to which you lost depended on your leverage or exposure down the credit quality.

There is a phrase that is used by my colleague Dan Fuss – "same bonds, different prices". He uses it when performance is exceptionally good as well as exceptionally poor. What he is saying here is that negative skewness, high kurtosis and fat tails associated with a liquidity crisis are not as worrisome. Where the bonds are "money good" you can expect a solid recovery. Yes, performance is poor but now you're earning a much higher yield spread and as the cycle improves or the crisis subsides you find yourself with good investments. Another way of thinking about this is that the downside risk as measured by semi-deviations tends to be exaggerated by a liquidity crisis. One of the sources of alpha is providing liquidity to an illiquid market (market timing). This may provide an opportunity to increase investment if the market is seeking liquidity.

Any upcoming changes in the tax or legal environment you deem important?

Yes, the upcoming US Pension Reforms, which need to be implemented whereby there is the need for marking to market. This means that long duration strategies (immunisation) will become more popular. Many sponsors are reluctant to immunise due to low interest rates or because their plan is underfunded at present. What is happening now is that they immunise their liabilities and then add a fixed-interest hedge fund or alpha overlay on top. We are already seeing customers move to the long-term government / credit long duration benchmark (11 to 12 years) or towards a benchmark more specifically representing their liability.

---

8 This means that you can expect many small gains, but also the occasional extreme drawdowns (fat tails). There may be substantial leverage involved. To maximise the small alpha inefficiencies in the fixed-interest market, arbitrageurs may need to leverage portfolios 10 to 20× and this creates problems when markets move against the positions in place. For this reason, some fund of hedge funds managers exclude fixed-interest strategies.

How do you see the industry evolving?

Some very large managers may have a harder time delivering alpha so we may see some additions to the industry leaders. I see more long short, alpha mandates, LDI mandates, more global mandates and global investors, but I also see a hedge fund fall out.

What keeps you busy outside of office hours?

Funny you should ask, I just completed my five-day test to become a Master (4th Dan) in the art of Tang Soo Do.[9] Martial arts have definitely helped my trading skills, in terms of its foundations in philosophy, psychology and discipline. To be one step ahead, to anticipate, and when to cut losses (laughs). Sun Tzu mentioned in *The Art of War*: "If you know the enemy and know yourself, you need not fear the result of a hundred battles."

Finally – bond investing in the future: art, science or skill?

All of the above – skill developed through science and art. I was talking to a Japanese plan sponsor who remarked that art is where you stop thinking, and was that what I meant by art? I answered no. I mean art in the sense of understanding human psychology, as it is a market run by humans. Back to martial arts: the markets are like a big fighting arena. There is a scientific method to it all, such as how to manage your balance, but it is the art that makes us humans indispensable, as we need to process information and be one step ahead of our opponents. So, yes although there are very useful quantitative approaches, I'm not a believer in a generalised pure quant approach.

Thank you for your time.

It is probably a fair comment that at present we are at the later stages of an economic expansion, while credit and higher yielding debt tend to perform best during the early stages of economic recovery. Despite the recent spike in yields due to the subprime

---

9   Tang Soo Do: a Korean martial art, also practised by Chuck Norris. Jae is also a 1st degree black belt in the art of Tae Kwon Do.

crisis, demand from institutional investors is likely to keep yields at relative historic lows unless inflation picks up significantly. At the same time, we expect continued development of the more exotic fixed-interest markets and structured products as investors demand higher income products. Apart from the historically high level of consumer debt, the corporate debt segment on the surface does not show signs of significant stress at this particular point in time.

As emphasised by the recent subprime crisis, several sources point to a number of warning signs:

- The ease of credit available to risky sectors.

- Inflated asset prices (especially property) may create inappropriate private and corporate balance sheets.

- The risk of moral hazard has increased after continued intervention by the Federal Reserve (for example, LTCM in 1998, September 11 in 2001, or during the recent subprime crisis).

- The complex credit system (especially the extensive use of credit derivatives) has never been stress tested.

- The source of easy funding from the yen carry trade (borrowing at zero interest rates) has dried up.

At this stage of the credit cycle, fixed interest may be less attractive as yields are low and the prospect of further capital gains is limited. Nevertheless, the downside risk in especially higher grade fixed interest is likely to be muted unless a severe decline in collateral values occurs. A skilled, opportunistic manager may still be able to add value, especially in the rotational credit and alpha transfer space.

PART V: WHERE TO FOR HEDGE FUND RETURNS?

7. TRENDS IN THE HEDGE FUND INDUSTRY

An interview with Blaine Tomlinson on
developments in the hedge fund industry

*"Markets are constantly in a state of uncertainty and flux and money
is made by discounting the obvious and betting on the unexpected."*
– George Soros[1]

INTRODUCTION

Hedge funds are attracting interest among both institutional and
retail investors due to their focus on absolute returns, the reliance
on skill (alpha) rather than markets (beta), and the alignment of
interests created as managers commit substantial sums of money to
the vehicles which they manage for clients.

Investors have been willing to compromise on fees, transparency and liquidity for the promise of desirable absolute returns.
However, the recent rapid increase in the supply of hedge funds
has raised a number of serious questions on the sustainability of
returns. Do we really need 10,000 hedge funds? Are hedge fund
managers worth their fees and do they protect us from severe loss
of capital as they promise?

---

1   Perhaps the most famous hedge fund manager of all times, George Soros is a
    Hungarian born billionaire hedge fund investor, philanthropist and author. He
    is best known as "The Man Who Broke the Bank of England" after shorting the
    Pound Sterling, believing it was overvalued. Soros earned US$1.1 billion in a single
    day from the deal in 1992.

Trends in the hedge fund industry

- *A flood of new managers.* Currently there are more than 9,500 funds collectively investing US$1.8 trillion. An estimated 100 to 150 new managers enter the market each month.

- *An increase in fees for superior managers.* While there is an abundance of manager supply, there is even more overwhelming demand for superior managers with 2 and 20[2] becoming their new standard fee structure.

- *Increased proactiveness from managers in the hunt for alpha.* Hedge funds are entering less liquid and private markets, initiate rather than react to deal flow, and utilise new instruments such as credit default swaps, enter new geographies such as Asian long short, and embrace market segments such as asset-backed lending.

- *Investors are increasingly thinking in terms of solutions, rather than products.* The separation of alpha and beta and the concept of portable alpha are gaining traction.[3] At the same time, it is being argued that the pure skill component in hedge funds may be smaller than it seems.[4] What is currently sold as alpha may become recognised as beta in the future, and may need to be sold at a lower price through index funds, futures, ETFs or swaps, while the fees for good quality pure alpha may increase.

- *Increased interest in single manager single-strategy and multi-strategy solutions.* A number of institutional investors have augmented their in-house expertise by establishing larger investment teams and are showing increased interest in diversifying from their initial fund of hedge funds exposure. They are showing interest in single manager single-strategy and multi-strategy products to reduce fees, increase transparency and optimise their overall portfolio risk and return objectives.

---

2   That is, a base fee of 2% of capital and an additional fee of 20% of performance, in many cases with no hurdle rate of return being required before the performance fee becomes payable.

3   In a portable alpha strategy, an investor seeks alpha in an asset class that may not form part of his/her desired long term strategic asset allocation (SAA) and uses futures or swaps to remove the risk of that market, replacing it with that reflecting the SAA.

4   Studies by Ibbotson and Bridgewater estimate that the actual skill involved may be less than half of the net of fee returns.

This section looks at the trends and factors involved for both single-strategy and multi-strategy hedge funds from an institutional and fund of hedge fund perspective.

Introducing Blaine Tomlinson

Blaine is Chairman of FRM (Financial Risk Management), a global fund of hedge funds that serves institutional investors. He founded the firm in 1991. Blaine originally grew up in South Africa and holds an MBA from the University of Cape Town. Blaine left South Africa in 1976 and moved to London with 500 South African rand (about $72) in his wallet and found a job working for Bank of America's leveraged-leasing group doing structured finance. Subsequently he worked for Citigroup, Nomura and AIG, trading and designing innovative investment products.

While busy trading, Blaine became interested in hedge fund managers and their ability to capture upside volatility while minimising downside risk. He and his wife Laura began gathering data and building spreadsheets. The idea for FRM was born as Blaine hired four young analysts, who worked in the attic of his Victorian house near London's Hampstead Heath, compiling statistics.

Nowadays, FRM has over 220 employees worldwide and is known to have one of the most extensive databases in the industry. FRM was selected by MSCI to help provide their hedge fund indices. FRM differentiate themselves by efficiently combining extensive quantitative analysis with thorough manager due diligence.

Blaine, thanks for your time. I would like to start off with some of your earlier work which I remember hit the media back in the late 1990s.[5] What are the main differences in the public perception of hedge funds when you compare the current time to back in 1998?

A decade ago, hedge funds were thought of as risky, leveraged speculators. When we first began marketing a fund in '98, it took a lot of convincing for institutions to take hedge funds seriously. When we studied the industry in the '90s, we saw that the best hedge fund

---

5 *The Financial Times* ran an article on August 11, 1998, titled "Hedge funds now revealed as great for widows and orphans", which was based on some of Blaine's earlier work, titled "Hedge funds demystified", co-authored with Goldman Sachs.

managers generated much more alpha than long-only managers because:

- They actively managed market risk and therefore were better at avoiding significant downside risk.

- As truly unconstrained active managers, they were free to invest in their best ideas and were not constrained by benchmarks.

As a result, hedge funds had better risk/return profiles than long-only funds. So we felt it was only a matter of time before institutions began to recognise this. And we knew we could build a business, building hedge fund portfolios for institutions.

What helped us was the joint article we published with Goldman Sachs. We had one of the most extensive databases of hedge funds and sophisticated hedge fund analytics, and we worked with Goldman to produce something that explained what hedge funds were doing, their different strategies and how they could be combined in ways that created attractive portfolios. After that paper, we found a lot more institutional interest. Among the first to invest were Japanese institutions, driven out of need for returns. Now we have over 200 pension fund clients, and hedge funds are considered by some of the more sophisticated institutions as "mainstream" allocations in their portfolios.

Did you get much negative response after the LTCM debacle hit in September 1998?

We had launched our first fund earlier that year, so our initial reaction was that perhaps we could have had better timing! Although we had no exposure to LTCM and had a positive return in '98, investors were shocked.

However, the bad publicity turned out to be good publicity for the industry. What LTCM did was elevate the discussion of hedge funds. Before that, when I spoke about hedge funds, it was Greek to most people. But after LTCM, everyone wanted to talk about hedge funds. Because we had amassed a huge amount of data on hedge funds, we were in a good position to educate investors.

This particularly helped us in Japan. I was spending a lot of time there and we were able to explain to the Japanese market what happened. That helped us develop those relationships as an educated investor.

Could such a thing happen again (a single event large enough to threaten a systemic collapse of the financial system)?[6]

First, the hedge fund industry has learned from LTCM. Risk controls are better, there is less leverage and prime brokers are more vigilant. However, dramatic fund collapses do happen and likely will continue to happen on occasion, especially when funds take aggressive risks and large positions in assets with moderate liquidity. Hedge funds do have risks, and that is why a diversified approach is crucial.

That being said, we don't see a big hedge fund collapse causing the sort of disruption that LTCM did. Amaranth actually lost more money, but barely affected the markets. For hedge funds to disrupt the markets, you'd have to have a group of funds whose positions are correlated all moving at the same time.

What do you think the main systemic risks to the financial system are today? (For example, terrorism, household debt, commodities, emerging markets.)

We focus very intently on a hedge fund manager's ability to navigate risk and to adapt to different market conditions. So our risk controls are not in making macroeconomic calls, but rather finding and investing in the managers who could best handle a financial system disruption. Hedge funds are frequently a source of liquidity for the markets. As a result they enable more efficient capital allocations and reduce overall market risk. This has shown up in reduced market volatility in recent years. What worries us more is a prime broker getting into trouble. If that happened, it could affect a large number of hedge funds, and thus the market. However, these institutions are prudently managed; and as 9/11 and the power outages in the US showed, they have fairly robust emergency backup procedures.

Are the authorities better placed now to handle such risks? Or worse?

---

6 Some people argue that the financial system now has become much more complex and less transparent, and that risk has not disappeared, but has merely been redistributed (for example, among the investment banks taking on the other side of, for example, emerging market debt through credit default swaps), and that hedge funds are attracting the same crowd as portfolio insurance did in 1987.

Regulators are much more educated about hedge funds and aware of their activities. They have a much higher level of dialogue with the industry. We get information calls from most major regulatory authorities such as the SEC, FSA and the Bank of England asking for input on industry issues. This increased dialogue gives us comfort that authorities are more educated on hedge funds, and would work with the industry to get through any problems.

What types of risk measurements do you consider most important when looking at hedge funds? Can quantitative methods adequately capture tail risk?

The critical point is that your risk is tomorrow's risk. Past data is helpful, but investors must know what risks a manager is taking today. Risks in markets can change very quickly. The volatility assumptions built into risk models are often based on historical levels, and it would be imprudent to think that market risk levels are constant – they are not.

The ultimate judge of risk is a qualitative one, but a lot of quantitative analysis goes into the qualitative judgement. Investors must establish the links between a manager's investment and risk management processes, market action and their performance. Returns are driven primarily by market opportunities, while risk management is a disciplined, skill-based process that tends to be persistent.

So downside volatility measures and Sortino ratios are valuable. Other measures tend to vary from sector to sector: VaR and stress-testing methodologies can be very useful in some relative value and directional trading strategies; net/gross balance sheet and sector/stock level detail is helpful in equity long-short. The key is to identify which normal and extreme market exposures a manager is intending to run, and then to agree on specific ranges of risk acceptable to the manager and to us as an investor.

What do you see as some of the key trends in the hedge fund industry?

- *There is a global movement towards more active, unconstrained investment management.* There will be continued growth in the number of managers, with the best new talent being attracted to the hedge fund industry. Innovation is unlikely to slow down.

Hedge funds strategies are becoming more diverse and, in the case of niche strategies, more difficult to evaluate.

- *Barriers to entry are increasing.* Investors require better infrastructure, trading strategies are now more complex, and it is harder for lesser known start-ups to raise capital. Development of seeding platforms will grow, as this may be a more attractive option than joining a multi-strategy firm.

- *Regulation is likely to increase* – not just from the investor protection side (securities regulators) but also potentially systematic risk (bank regulators).

- *There is enormous pressure from investors for increased transparency*, even up to position level. For many managers their strategies and positions are proprietary. This will continue to be an ongoing debate. I suspect that increased transparency is inevitable as the industry grows up.

- *Hedge funds are increasingly taking on bank lending roles.* For them, it is an attractive investment, as these loans are high up in the capital structure, have shorter durations and are floating rate. The increasing growth of hedge funds as liquidity providers in markets complements the regulated banking system. The large multi-strategy funds are already starting to look like investment banks. Increasingly they do market making, direct lending, new issues and through activism are involved in M & A. The only missing part is sales.

- *Funds of funds will continue to grow*, because they add value as they enable investors to tap the highly complex, constantly changing hedge fund market and provide access to hard-to-generate alpha. They also provide effective portfolio construction, diversification and monitoring and generate attractive net returns to investors.

What is the impact of the institutionalisation of the hedge fund industry?

The recent Casey Quirk study predicted that institutional assets in hedge funds will triple by 2010, which points to increasing acceptance. But it's not just a number – alternative investing is changing how institutions look at their portfolios, and in turn institutional requirements are guiding the development of the hedge fund industry.

Institutional allocations to hedge funds are increasing from a low base – particularly public and corporate pension funds. I believe the US will represent the single largest source of flows, followed by Japan, Continental Europe and the UK. In terms of asset size of hedge funds, as they get bigger, returns do diminish. This is a real issue in the hedge fund industry. Some of the larger hedge funds are more focused on asset gathering than generating returns. Smaller funds are more nimble, and are more likely to produce outsized returns if you can find the right ones.

At the strategy level, the best opportunities are in equity and credit strategies, where alpha is not a zero-sum game. Long-only and hedge funds investors are often looking at quite different opportunities and have very different risk objectives and utility functions. Over time, sector hedge funds will be included in the mainstream asset allocations of institutions.

I think that diversified portfolios of hedge funds will be used as the alpha engine for portable alpha solutions. Also, as LDI becomes more mainstream so will the high-quality risk-adjusted returns of hedge funds become better recognised. Having said all that, competition for large mandates is fierce and the RFP process is complex. Funds of funds require substantial experience and investment in sales and marketing to compete. Institutional investors nowadays expect "feet on the ground" in key global financial markets – to source managers and to provide client coverage.

Have you any views on the economic environment and how this will affect hedge fund returns going forward?

We don't overly focus on macroeconomic calls; we run our entire portfolio through three broad scenarios: stable, risk-seeking and risk-aversion. Our analysts estimate the returns of each of our underlying funds in those scenarios, and we analyse the performance of the portfolio of the whole. Then we try to adjust our portfolios to deliver acceptable returns to our clients under all scenarios.

As investors, our ability to make short-term market timing calls is limited because of liquidity provisions of managers. What we do, however, is to focus on shorter term opportunities in specific sectors with specific managers, and increase allocations there. We strongly believe that one of the major benefits of investing in hedge funds is the ability of managers to adapt to changing macroeconomic conditions. When there is new information, they adapt their thinking.

One final observation I'll share is that longer term, the overall hedge fund opportunity set is best when you have high levels of government intervention, corporate activity and investor inefficiency. These three "alpha" creators are becoming more active and overall return levels appear to be on the rise.

Do we really need 10,000 hedge fund managers? How many would you deem worthy of further research?

Do we need 10,000 managers? While having less managers might make it easier for those of us who select them, it also may mean less creativity and entrepreneurialism in hedge funds. There is a natural attrition rate in hedge funds. Only the best grow and thrive over the long term. The lowest quality managers will inevitably close their funds, and so will – I suspect – many average managers.

There are probably no more than 1,000 serious hedge fund groups. However, it takes a lot of time to cover that entire universe of 10,000 funds to find the 1,000 or so worth seriously considering. We have a large investment staff on a global basis which spends significant time doing just that.

There are several thousand average-to-poor managers with small amounts of assets under management, who have no real hope of becoming successful asset management businesses.

What will their impact be on the overall alpha pie?

As assets continue to grow, expected returns going forward are likely to decrease, as more money is thrown at fewer opportunities. It will become harder and harder to generate excess alpha. This is a real issue for individual hedge funds. Also, generating alpha may become more complex.

Hedge fund managers are typically entrepreneurial and innovative. They are frequently the first managers into new investment strategies. Hedge funds are for the most part investing in the same asset classes as long-only managers – although not necessarily in the same stocks. The flexibility that hedge funds have to invest in their best ideas rather than in a constrained universe will mean that regardless of the market conditions, the best hedge funds will generate more alpha than long-only managers. Long-only alpha is more constrained, and for many long-only managers is a zero-sum game. I would say hedge fund alpha is far more abundant, especially for research-oriented equity and credit strategies.

Our observation is that fees are going up for the good managers to 2 and 20 and about half of them are closed. Do you concur with that? Are the managers worth this sort of fee?

We have no expectation that fees for the best and most successful managers will be coming down. As long as they have more assets than capacity, they have the ability to charge higher fees and impose longer lockups. However, only a small number of managers are permanently closed to all investors, though many of the best managers are closed to the majority of new investors. That's why it is increasingly important to be an early investor – otherwise you can't get capacity over time.

Newer managers will be subject to increasing fee pressure as institutional investors become a larger proportion of the investor base. *In fact, we're seeing fees come down a bit for newer managers.* Head line fees are often an issue for the first-time investor in hedge funds. However, if we analyse fees in the context of "active risk" and compare the "active risk" that hedge funds take compared to the active risk that most long managers take, hedge fund fees start to look more reasonable. For example, if a long-only manager charges, say, 50 to 75 basis points for managing their portfolio, this equates very broadly to a 1.5% to 2% fee for hedge funds. When you take into account that the best hedge funds constrain their capacity and are more focused on return generation than asset growth, the overall fees, including performance fees, seem – at least to me – to be more reasonable.

Are managers worth this fee? Since hedge funds are measured and compared on returns net of fees, if their gross returns are so good that net returns are still exceptional, then clearly as an investor you would be willing to pay those fees. For institutional investors, other issues sometimes come ahead of fees, including the quality of returns, the quality and depth of the people and organisation, and the quality of the risk management process including the operational risk processes. Institutions are often most concerned about head line risk.

In general, do you have a preference for quantitative or qualitative techniques for screening? Are most of your new candidates still from prime broker, client and investment bank referrals?

We find managers through a variety of sources – there is no one way to find managers other than through hard work and resources. What is becoming more common is to be on the second or third generation of managers who spin out of other managers. Quantitative techniques can only be applied when there is a fairly long track record – and in this environment, you must be an early investor in order to get capacity in the best managers. However, we constantly compare our invested managers to their peer groups using quantitative techniques, and this does lead us to new opportunities from time to time. We use quantitative techniques more extensively for manager monitoring and portfolio construction.

What are some of the new strategies/instruments/ developments in the hedge funds space that you get excited about?

Hedge funds remain the most entrepreneurial asset managers applying modern-day risk management techniques to existing asset classes and are actively involved in developing new areas of investment. The rate of innovation has not slowed and is unlikely to slow down. Some new strategies we've reviewed include carbon emissions trading, energy trading, life settlements, securitised emerging market mortgages, trade receivables, middle market lending and catastrophe bonds, and some of these styles have found their way into our portfolios.

We are constantly on the hunt for new strategies and are open to any strategy where sufficient market opportunities and liquidity exists and where managers can demonstrate a repeatable, scaleable process to generate returns. However, many of the newer strategies don't meet those requirements. The strategies that do tend to be attractive are new managers trading core markets. For example, the credit sector has really blossomed over the past few years, with an explosion of products, markets and trading styles. So have some of the "emerged" markets, such as some found in Asia, Latin America and Eastern Europe.

Recently there has been a lot of debate on factor neutrality, an anti-beta bias, and the reconstruction of hedge fund alpha though multi-factor regression modelling. What are your thoughts on the whole "hedge fund returns are easy to replicate and we want alpha only" debate?

One thing to bear in mind is that multi-factor regression modelling does not capture hedge fund alpha. Rather, it captures hedge fund beta. Therefore, the key question is why would one want to pay for hedge fund beta without getting the alpha as well?

Hedge funds are meant to produce excess absolute returns using the best means available and with limited drawdowns. So hedge funds that correlate highly with primary markets or risk premia are a cause for concern. Replicating strategies are backward looking which means that they are always late in adjusting to the market. By using monthly rebalancing, they are not nimble enough to adapt to a changing market environment. Replicating strategies also do not offer risk management/balance sheet management. While risk management is not the primary source of alpha in hedge funds, it nevertheless is an important source of alpha – if you can control your risk, you can lever your portfolio more and improve your risk/reward profile. Therefore, replicating strategies may produce higher returns at a lower cost in stable environments, but there is no loss limitation on the down side. Over long periods they will trade at low Sharpe ratios.

Some hedge fund strategies have a propensity to do better in good equity environments (without necessarily doing very badly in bad markets). Funds of funds address this issue: they build portfolios which can offset this asymmetry – that can be challenging and it can be as important a part of the service as picking good managers. It may not be a coincidence that issues such as replicating strategies, which are aimed at undermining the hedge fund industry, are gaining in popularity at a time when we are about three years into an equity market bull run. If investors do not believe that hedge funds are a good proposition, why would you want to replicate them? Why not just stay away from hedge funds altogether? *Remember that it's hard to compare replicators or index trackers to active funds because active funds have additional constraints such as beta, Libor plus targets, so you'd be comparing apples to oranges.*

With more and more managers using similar portfolios in terms of strategies, we have noticed that the dispersion between the successful and the unsuccessful fund of fund managers has become less and less. How do you think fund of hedge fund managers can continue to differentiate themselves?

One point of differentiation is in products that target specific sectors of the hedge fund industry, and in that area we (and others) have produced performance that stands out. However, regarding the broadly diversified portfolios that funds of funds also offer, the real strength of most portfolios can only be measured in a crisis. In recent years, the correlation between strategies was high. Therefore, there wasn't much difference among funds of funds based on differences in their portfolio construction. However, the only thing constant about market environments is that they are never constant. We've built our diversified portfolios to target consistent returns across all market environments, and so we have heavier allocations to trading strategies that perform well during turbulence. Returns aside, investors need to look at the process and infrastructure of the managers, because that is what they are buying. Also, funds of funds like ours have become much more client-focused, and have customised products to meet specific investor needs.

Fund of funds' scale matters and will become an increasing differentiator amongst fund of funds firms. I believe the largest firms will continue to get a disproportionate share of new flows because of their ability to:

- Invest in the required infrastructure (due diligence, sales and marketing).

- Attract and retain the best talent.

- Serve key institutional accounts.

- Develop new products and customise client solutions.

- Access top hedge funds.

Hence, I think organic growth will continue to be strong for the best funds of funds.

How important do you rate manager selection versus strategy allocation in terms of contribution to returns for funds of hedge funds?

Each is important, but they are difficult to compare because each has a different goal and purpose. Manager selection is clearly crucial. We devote enormous resources globally to evaluate, select and monitor managers. The goal is to select managers who can produce alpha on a consistent basis. Long term, that is the most crucial component of returns.

The purpose of strategy allocation is to blend these managers together to create portfolios with target return profiles. For example, our diversified portfolios are designed to have 0 beta to the S&P 500 – so that determines our strategy allocation. Strategy allocation is more of a risk control mechanism. Strategy allocation also is intrinsically part of the manager selection process. When we weight managers in portfolios, we are also weighting the opportunities presented by their sectors. So in the near term, our investment pool is weighted towards managers with the largest alpha generation potential. A final point is that increasingly investors are attracted to products that offer them specific strategy exposure – thus the issue of strategy allocation becomes a moot point when we offer targeted exposure to what we think are the best of breed managers in a sector.

Have you any comments on the growing listed fund of hedge funds market? Would FRM be interested in listing its funds or itself?[7]

Our firm was built to serve institutional investors, which tend to be most demanding, and that will continue to be the bulk of our business. However, as one of the larger fund of funds, we do have a diverse product base, some of which may be appropriate for listing. We already have one listed fund, and over time there may be others. In terms of listing FRM, we're doing quite well as a privately held firm.

---

7   Listing has some potential benefits such as improved pricing and liquidity, as well as better access for retail clients.

How do you see competition from the multi-strategy players evolving?[8]

There are significant differences between multi-strategy firms and funds of funds, and there will continue to be a place for both, depending upon investor concerns.

*   Multi-strategy firms sit between single-strategy and funds of funds on the risk spectrum. The number of strategies they employ aren't as diverse as in a fund of funds, and you still have the business risk of an organisational collapse or a failure in risk management. So, yes the returns of a multi-strategy can sometimes exceed a diversified fund of funds, but you're also accepting a higher level of risk than a diversified fund of funds. Multi-strategy managers are in essence just a collection of single-strategy managers owned by one firm, and the advantage is that a multi-strategy manager can allocate capital quickly between them. The problem is that the quality of each single strategy team can vary, and the best traders often want to leave and start their own funds.

*   A fund of funds essentially selects the best of breed managers in each sector, with the philosophy that you want complete flexibility to choose the best managers out of a large universe. Also, the diversity of managers and strategies in large funds of funds exceeds that of multi-strategy funds.

The fee question is one where I differ from common industry understanding. Most multi-strategy firms have higher fee levels than single-strategy managers. If you go the direct approach and add the additional expense of hiring professionals to select and monitor these firms, and the higher potential for loss, the fund of funds will be the more cost-efficient option in many cases. That is, *many people forget that in order for multi-strategy funds to properly diversify, the cost of bringing in the additional expertise may mean the fees can go up to 5% to 8% of returns, which is not always reported through the management fee, but rather is included as a cost of business.*

---

8   Cost is an issue for funds of funds, which typically charge management fees of 1.0% and incentive fees of 10% on top of the fees charged by the managers in which they invest. In difficult economic environments the extra layer of fees can swiftly erode the net returns for investors, and some investors are exploring ways to avoid the second layer of fees. In addition to designing their own portfolios of direct investments, some institutions are choosing to work with the larger multi-strategy firms.

What are the differences in hedge fund appetite of investors in the different regions? Are hedge funds still mainly seen as a bond substitute for liability-driven investment?

The differences in product demand among regions can largely be traced to the length of time institutional investors have been invested in hedge funds. Generally speaking, pension funds and insurance companies tend to prefer lower volatility, lower correlation to equities-type products. That type of product is often the first style of product that any investor wants to buy. As investors become more accustomed to hedge funds, they tend to ask for more concentrated sector products. So we've evolved our product line to include higher risk, more concentrated products. However, we've found this evolutionary process among institutional investors to be fairly consistent around the world.

How do you see the investment industry in 10 years time, in particular the role of hedge funds?

The term "hedge fund" may not exist. We will most likely be in a world where there are truly active managers which charge higher fees, and truly passive managers with low fees. I think there will be a push toward larger, more diversified firms with returns that are lower from a historical perspective but still attractive.

The largest hedge funds and the largest traditional managers may end up looking a lot like each other. However, there will always be a major role for nimble specialists who deploy significant capital and produce outsized returns, and for the pure alpha generator which finds a way to make money outside the established structure. As a fund of funds, our role will continue to be as an institutional quality asset manager, but one that finds these nimble, entrepreneurial alpha generators, and constructs portfolios of them to reduce risks and provide extremely attractive return streams to our institutional clients.

What keeps you occupied outside of work?

When I was young I enjoyed surfing. For a while I ran marathons too; my last one was in 1986.[9] My passions today outside of investing are heli-skiing (I recently went to Canada with my three sons

---

9 Blaine used to be an avid marathon runner. His personal best is two hours and 40 minutes, a time beyond the reach of all but the best club runners.

and really enjoy this), sailing and hiking. I spend most of my spare time reading about and studying markets – which for many people might seem quite boring. If I hadn't been in this industry, my other passion would be psychology and human behaviour.

Finally – hedge fund investing in the future: would you consider it an art, science or skill?

Clearly all three elements are at play – but I'd say it is primarily a skill. The skill lies in executing a methodical and repeatable process. It is consistently making investments that have a better-than-average chance of paying off. The best managers have that ability – they have identified processes that work. For a fund of fund manager there is an art as well. To pick the best managers, we need to be good "readers" of people.

Thank you for your time.

Blaine's primary interest when assessing hedge funds remains on risk management. Managers need to prove that they are capable of controlling downside risk, no matter how good they are in generating alpha. In some ways, Blaine likes to compare FRM to the six-inch high, hand-carved wooden hippopotamus that stands in his office. Though they may seem slow and complacent, they can move at remarkable speed.

From an investor's perspective, it pays to be aware that fund of hedge fund returns may depend on a number of external factors affecting total returns, as well as the return dispersions between the different managers[10]:

- The level of bullishness in the equity markets.

- The level of capital market volatility.

- The increased focus on risk, reducing bet size and manager concentration.

- The reduced leverage, on average now 1 to 3×.

- The increased competition.

---

10 Liem, H, and D Timotijevic, November 2005, *Survival of the Fittest*, Mercer Investment Consulting.

When assessing funds of hedge funds, investors will need to examine the breadth of strategies employed, whether strong operational and investment due diligence teams exist, and whether risk management is undertaken on a transparent basis. At the same time we are already seeing a number of managers develop single-manager single-strategy and multi-strategy products and solutions to cater for the increased demand from clients for removal of the second layer of fees, increased transparency, higher liquidity and the right mix of alpha and beta within their overall portfolios.

8. THE PARADOX OF PASSIVE ALPHA

An interview with Oliver Schupp on
Passive Hedge Funds management

*"How wonderful that we have met with a paradox.
Now we have some hope of making progress."*
– Niels Bohr (1885–1962)

INTRODUCTION

The word paradox is often used interchangeably and wrongly with contradiction; but whereas a contradiction asserts its own opposite, many paradoxes do allow for resolution of some kind, as long as the observer is able to question the original premises. Can the philosophies of alpha and the benefits of passive management be successfully combined?

Passive hedge fund investing

Indexing has been an ideal method of getting low-cost exposure, especially to some of the traditionally more efficient markets. A lively debate has evolved around hedge fund *indexing* (mimicking active hedge fund manager indices) and hedge fund *cloning* (replicating returns from hedge fund factors), so as to do away with the second layer of fees charged by funds of hedge funds. Tomeo et al (2005) arrive at several conclusions:

- Hedge fund indices provide a valuable service in attempting to quantify the performance of various hedge fund styles, and typically provide a level of transparency and liquidity over and above that of most funds of funds. However, their success in doing so varies significantly from one index provider to another, and is primarily a function of index composition and rules-based methodology.

- There are both theoretical and practical barriers to implementing an index approach in the hedge fund universe. Practically speaking, hedge fund indices are difficult to create, maintain, and replicate. Also, there are challenges to creating investable, liquid vehicles for investors. In addition, while modern portfolio theory provides a solid theoretical justification for passive investment in the "market portfolio" of investable securities, research has yet to determine whether this is valid when applied to a universe of hedge fund managers.

Despite the lack of theoretical underpinnings, hedge fund "index" products exist and continue to proliferate and evolve. These products may appeal to investors because they address some of the most problematic elements of hedge fund investing, provide a potential source of liquidity and achieve greater levels of transparency.

Indexing versus cloning

Before we can claim that hedge fund indices can be successfully tracked, we need to understand the techniques being used. A number of issues remain unresolved.

Indexing:

- Fees may be *1% on top* of the usual 2% + 20% fees charged by the active managers underlying the index. Compare this to active fees where a major client may actually be paying 1% + 10% for an active FoHF manager.

- Some research indicates that investable indices tend to underperform the broader aggregate (non-investable) indices. Apart from the differences in asset allocation and index methodology, some commentators have attributed this to survivorship bias. We will expand on this during our interview and examine whether these comments are justified.

- There is some research indicating that *the total amount of alpha (as defined by "non-replicable" by factor analysis) may be coming down.* Hence this could affect any index of "active managers".

- Despite all this, we note that there are some products out there that have successfully tracked the broader non-investable aggregate indices with actual risk-adjusted returns superior to a number of FoHF over a multi-year period. The tracking techniques have been proven in traditional asset classes, though we note that index investing in active managers, rather than asset classes, may be subject to access to liquidity of the underlying manager.

Cloning:

- Fees are between 1% minimum (for a passive clone) to 1.5% + 15% without hurdle (for an active clone). This is *a single layer of fees.*

- Cloning may be considered a form of active management; that is, even passive clones may show substantial difference to index performance, as the cloning concept has only recently started. Most of these clones have a limited performance history, with most only started by late 2006 or early 2007. This does not prove anything about the stability of the factors.

- Estimates of the systematic portion of alpha vary between 50% and 80% being cloneable through factors.

- Some of the active clones engage in non-linear distribution replication (that is, using forward-looking trading rules) rather than linear replication, even adding security selection. In this case, the clone is bordering on the fringe of global macro/multi-strategy managers, possibly without regard to risk, return or beta considerations.

- Some of the more interesting strategies such as market neutral or distressed debt have proven inherently difficult to clone.

- *There is a major academic debate going on as to what extent the weights to the different factors will remain stable going forward.*

Introducing Oliver Schupp

Oliver Schupp is a Managing Director of Credit Suisse in the Asset Management division, based in New York. He is President of Credit Suisse/Tremont Index LLC. He also has responsibility for product development and oversight of investments for the index-linked product suite. Oliver joined Credit Suisse First Boston in

April 2000 from Commerzbank Securities in London, where he was a trader for the Program Trading and Index Arbitrage team, and a portfolio analyst in the quantitative research team. Prior to that, Oliver worked at BARRA in Frankfurt and London as a Senior Consultant, where he advised international money managers in risk management, optimisation and asset allocation models. Oliver holds a Masters in Economics specialising in Finance, Accounting and Public Finance from Johannes Gutenberg University in Mainz, Germany. Oliver is Series 3, 17, 63 licensed. He is the Chairman of the Credit Suisse/Tremont Hedge Fund Index Committee. We asked Oliver about the pros and cons of passive hedge fund investment.

Oliver, thank you for your time. You worked at Barra for a number of years. What do you find to be the main differences when trying to index "active managers", rather than asset classes?

Our hedge fund indices seek similar goals and apply similar construction methodologies to that of traditional indices, which have proven and commonly accepted standards. Asset classes behave typically more homogenously with identifiable characteristics and associated risk premiums. Hedge funds invest in existing asset classes and are able to change their allocations on an opportunistic basis and as such are more dynamic and heterogeneous in nature. An index measures the average return experienced by its constituents while providing a mode of comparison to the performance of the industry.

Hedge fund indexing *diverges* from traditional indices in the amount of effort involved in calculating and maintaining the indices. For example, manager data is not as readily available as the exchange-traded instruments used by typical asset class indices. *In any case, there is still an active academic debate as to whether hedge funds are representative of the underlying assets they invest in or simply an asset class in themselves.* Considering hedge fund indices do capture manager-specific alpha, it is safe to say that indexing active managers achieves the same goals as creating an index of the constituents of a more traditional index.

Could you for the benefit of our readers compare and contrast indexing versus cloning. Is there one you favour over the other, and why?

Cloning has recently emerged as several well-known banks have launched products in this new segment of hedge fund investing. The sudden emergence and discussion of such products solidifies and strengthens our position that passively managed portfolios provide an increasingly attractive investment alternative to actively managed portfolios. In particular indexation sees healthy demand in the recent past which is part coming from the fee debate but also attractive and comparable returns of indices versus their active counterparts.

- *Indexation* is based on investments into the underlying securities (funds) that constitute the index. As such, index products express the aggregate characteristics of the hedge funds. Valuation and liquidity is typically not as high as with clones, though we have several exchange-traded products with daily or intraday liquidity.

- *Cloning*, by contrast, is an attempt to identify common (tradable) market factors and as such synthetically replicate the return stream of hedge fund (index) returns. *The main difference is that there is no investment into the underlying hedge funds and as such the manager fees of 2/20 are avoided.* In addition, given the investment in liquid common market factors these products may offer daily valuations, liquidity and a high level of transparency. *Academics argue that the savings in fees could be offset by the loss of manager-specific alpha.*

Indexing is a great way to gain access to a representative sample of hedge funds capturing all returns generated by those funds, while none of the clones argue that they are able to capture the manager-specific alpha. Clones are still young and will have to prove that they are capable of achieving their goals.

It is probably fair to say that clones, although untested, represent an avenue to alternative beta, while indexing encompasses that but also includes an alpha element. How do you see the alpha and beta contributions for hedge funds going forward? I'm sure you're familiar

with, for example, the work of Dr Lars Jaeger who argues the non-systematic part of returns is coming down? Would you agree that the hedge fund market is becoming more "alternative beta" efficient?

I am indeed familiar with the interesting work of Dr Jaeger and his approach to alternative beta. Since it is believed that a rising number of hedge funds have crowded many successful strategies and diminished the manager-specific alpha in those sectors, it seems logical that alternative beta as discussed by Dr Jaeger has driven some hedge fund returns. In addition, other research by Fung/Hsieh and Lo has shown significant elements of common market factors in hedge fund returns and contributed to this debate. This should not come as a surprise as hedge funds invest in other asset classes to start with.

And, it is well observed and noted that the hedge fund industry is facing challenges every time markets don't show any sustainable trends over a prolonged period of time. This can further be seen with the increasing correlations of hedge funds with the equity markets over the recent years and big gains when, for example, commodity and emerging markets have shown trends of several months. Investors have certainly become more aware of the high management and performance fees they pay for average returns, and a double layer of such fees with funds of funds. This sensitivity to fees is probably the single most important factor that has led to the rise of clones and a more perceptive environment for indexation. *I believe that the industry will go through a cycle where fees will have to be adjusted to meet performance standards. Successful funds may charge more than many of the low performers that will have to adjust their fees downward. This may lead to a flight of talent and an increased number of funds closing. Once this shakeout is complete, the percentage of manager-specific alpha in the industry might rise again.*

One often heard comment is that investable hedge fund indices tend to underperform due to survivorship bias, etc. How much of the first statement is true due to differences in asset allocation and how much is due to pure survivorship bias? Are there any other reasons for the discrepancy in performance?

- It is first important to point out that our investable index is not meant to track the broad index. It is a blue chip index focusing on the largest hedge funds that are open for new investments and provide certain liquidity criteria. Investable and broad indices, such as the Credit Suisse/Tremont Blue Chip Investable Index ("Investable Blue Chip") and the Credit Suisse/Tremont Hedge Fund Index ("Broad Index"), are often compared to one another, and many people may speculate on the differences in returns. Our Blue Chip Investable and Broad indices are constructed differently in terms of constituents and asset allocations.

- While the difference in the allocation to the individual strategies is easy to follow, the differences derived from the constituent funds are not as obvious. Investable indices require funds to be open and meet certain criteria such as liquidity. The broad indices include both open and closed funds, are not subject to liquidity constraints, and are designed to be representative of the entire industry. The result is that investable indices are representative of the current investment opportunities of funds that meet certain liquidity and additional requirements.

- *Survivorship bias is an often misunderstood criticism of hedge fund indices.* It is most prevalent in databases and research carried out on that data. *To the extent indices do not properly address survivorship bias in their construction it is of course a legitimate concern.*[1]

You manage to track the non-investable index quite closely. How do you sidestep survivorship bias (hedge fund blowups, etc.)? For example, monthly rebalancing? The clone proponents would say they'd never get stuck in an Amaranth, for example.

---

1 For an index this means that when calculating backwards funds that subsequently went out of business but would have qualified at the point in time also need to be included. The performance of funds that "die" needs to stay in the index. Survivorship bias is a matter of the index construction; neither traditional nor hedge fund indices should permit a survivorship bias to build up. As a guideline, any index should have objective and clear index rules describing the addition and deletion of member funds at the rebalance and should disallow the retrospective change of historical index performance, thus eliminating survivorship bias in its index construction. All funds that report to an index at the beginning of the index's reporting period should not be removed from the historical returns for any reason.

We employ proven portfolio model concepts that allow us to track the index fairly closely and we are doing this now for over five years. Hedge fund blowups can and will occur within indices and the tracking portfolios, however the effects of such blowups are generally limited due to the relative size of each position within the index or portfolio. In other words, the vast diversification of the portfolio limits the impact. In addition, monthly reviews and frequent rebalancing ensure positions do not grow more than a representative size within index tracking portfolios.

Why do clients still buy the investable indices if they know they underperform the non-investable indices?

It should be noted that often actively managed funds of funds criticise the non-investable index as performing too "good" because of biases yet the very same group attacks investable indices for not delivering the performance of the non-investable counterpart. You can't have it both ways. In addition, as mentioned earlier our investable index is not meant to track the broad index, it's a representative blue chip index.[2] For the tracking part we have a separate and very successful product. In contrast, many of the broad indices do not offer index tracking products, which may provide interesting alternatives for institutional investors. Our own tracking portfolio currently has a 98% correlation to our non-investable broad index and is running since July 2002.

You basically use the same techniques for indexing as would a normal passive manager to minimise its tracking error. What additional constraints do you face when using active managers rather than traditional assets; for example, in terms of selection and capacity?

We face several constraints including: managers can be closed to new or additional investment; investment and redemption capacities may be limited; subscription and redemption frequencies may vary; and investment and redemption minimums can be prohibitive.

---

2   Oliver mentions that well-constructed investable indices provide investors with a variety of positive features, including: predictability in the portfolio construction, liquidity, transparency, and the possibility to create a number of derivative structures, plus sometimes regulatory advantages. They are usually made up of fewer funds in an effort to maintain liquidity. They can still provide attractive risk-adjusted returns and in particular low volatility.

These constraints may lead to tracking error in the portfolio, but with sound optimisation techniques, the effect can be minimised. Our modelling tools take these constraints into consideration throughout the allocation process.

I understand your firm is coming out with clone products too. It is probably fair to say that clones are less constrained in terms of capacity, as they mainly use more liquid index futures, rather than (at times closed) managers with more limited capacity. Have you ever considered adding some parts of the cloning process to your indexing strategy to enhance either capacity or liquidity?

We are currently researching hedge fund replication and alternative beta strategies. If simple, liquid tradable factors are used as part of a replication product, then the benefits of the liquidity and capacity could potentially be a good complement for hedge fund indices and hedge fund of fund products. *What is reasonably clear is that the majority of academics and product providers all agree that the current theories/products only replicate a portion of hedge fund returns and that the unexplained portion of returns is effectively a cost of the high levels of liquidity and transparency potentially gained.*

Which strategies would you consider most difficult to index or replicate?

- Replication: there are numerous theories and methodologies, but as none of them have any significant live data or out of sample testing, it is difficult to exactly determine these strategies. *However, the majority of back-testing shows that equity long/short and parts of the event-driven sector investing seemed easiest to replicate using regression and mechanical modelling, while fixed-income arbitrage and equity market neutral tended to be more difficult to replicate.* It must be noted that there is no consensus on these findings and that depending on the methodologies applied and the factors chosen the results may significantly vary.

- In terms of indexing, there is no one sector that is most difficult to index. Sectors with fewer funds, many closed funds, or illiquid strategies can be hard to track. However, there are usually enough funds in every sub-sector such that hedge fund indices are sufficiently trackable.

What sort of client is most likely to index hedge funds?

- *Very sophisticated clients with longstanding experience in hedge fund investing and the intention to access a core multi-strategy position more cost-efficiently with an index without compromising returns.* Active managers are then often added as alpha source through either strategy-specific allocations or single-manager investments.

- *Second, retail investors who prefer an objective, transparent approach rather than relying on a fund of funds manager's skill set.* By comparing hedge fund investing to traditional asset classes, I would argue that any investor who is currently buying index products on the traditional side, including enhanced indexing or ETFs, would be likely buyers for hedge fund index products. We often hear that we are competing for the client's core investment in this asset class. These investors seek broad exposure to the asset class and at the same time want to limit any administrative burden. We have clients in over 25 countries on all continents, ranging from retail investors to large government pension plans, so I believe this shows that indexing is really suitable to a diverse range of investors.

What do you think of listed FoHF (closed ended or open ended) in this space as an alternative source of daily liquidity?

Listed investment vehicles utilise a different mode of raising assets. Investors should consider the differences of such an investment before being tempted by the potentially high levels of liquidity offered.[3] In several of these products, trading volume is moderate. On the other hand, these vehicles provide a possibility for investors that operate in higher regulated markets to gain access to managers that they might not otherwise have gained access to.

How do you see fee levels in the hedge fund space? The consensus seems to be that fees will be going up – especially for the good managers – due to the overwhelming demand.

---

3   In an open-ended fund, the investment manager manages the overall liquidity of the product in a way that would satisfy any possible redemption, limiting the investment horizon and the funds available to invest in. Due to offer and demand the pricing of closed-ended funds could, for example, show a discrepancy to similar products that are not listed and trade at a premium or discount.

Consistently top performing managers will always be able to attract investors at higher than average fee levels. On the other hand, I do not believe that fee levels will increase on average, as the average manager will not be able to demand higher compensation. Crowding within certain strategies and competition may drive down average fee levels over time. In addition, increased sophistication and experience will lead to fee pressure firstly on funds of funds which have to legitimate their double layer of fees.

What sort of transparency do you require from the underlying managers? Would the due diligence be similar to FoHF? For example, do you monitor style drift, etc.?

Each underlying manager must first provide a copy of their prospectus, historical monthly net performance and assets since inception, and a copy of the most recent audited financial statements. Once approved for inclusion in the broad index, we require all underlying hedge funds to submit monthly performance and asset information. For our investable indices, in addition to the monthly updates, we also ask for more frequent performance estimates and require a rigorous operational due diligence check before they can join the investable indices. We may also receive additional monthly reporting information of the hedge fund's activities and underlying exposure. On an ongoing basis, the hedge funds' trading style, strategy and performance are monitored both on a qualitative and quantitative basis.

Given the rather less liquid nature of hedge funds, what kind of liquidity and valuations can investors expect for passive indexing and cloning products?

Let's separate between liquidity and valuation. Indexation can offer daily liquidity as our products listed at several exchanges (SWX, Deutsche Börse Freiverkehr, and the Vienna Exchange) show, while valuation if not based on managed accounts is likely to be less frequent. It is important to understand what you receive for increased liquidity. In cloning, investors gain exposure to a mix of traditional assets that attempt to offer similar risk/return characteristics to hedge fund indices, not the hedge funds indices themselves.

Investors in these products must be prepared to potentially give up manager-specific alpha while enjoying higher levels of transparency and liquidity.

What sort of returns can investors expect from passive hedge fund indices?

The level of returns generated by hedge funds in the long run is very difficult to predict. However, returns of the Broad Index should reflect those of the overall hedge fund industry. Returns of the investable indices should reflect returns of the largest investable hedge funds of our Broad Index. Investors in a passive portfolio tracking product should expect returns similar to that of the index that it is designed to track.

In your opinion, how much percentage of their portfolios should investors allocate to passive hedge funds?

A core multi-strategy fund of fund position can be replaced more cost-efficiently with an index tracking fund without compromising on returns. In most portfolios this level does not exceed 10%, so perhaps half of that position can be replaced. Investors on average allocate a small amount of their overall portfolio, about 5% to 15%, to hedge fund strategies in an attempt to capture alpha which other investment strategies do not do. However, investors who allocate to many FoHF may be creating their own quasi-index and could certainly generate more efficient returns by simply investing in a passive hedge fund index and supplementing that investment with high alpha managers as satellites.

Has there been any interest in transporting the "alpha + beta" combination you get from passive hedge fund indices?

Absolutely. A few firms have now launched portable alpha products. Once you have a vehicle for transporting alpha, you can make many combinations of unique products by transporting the alpha onto any number of more traditional investment platforms like the S&P or ASX. As for transporting beta or alternative beta, some of our clients have chosen to transport alternative beta on a traditional index.

Back to our paradox: can passive management and alpha be successfully combined?[4]

I believe that aggregating hedge funds into an index will maintain an exposure to manager-specific alpha. Admittedly, there will be beta components to the index and industry, but nevertheless passive management can successfully deliver alpha of the underlying hedge funds to investors. An index of alpha-generating hedge funds should, by definition, still pass on alpha to an index investor.

What keeps you busy outside of office hours?

Outside the office, my 18-month-old daughter Sophia keeps me quite busy. In my spare time, I am an avid tri-athlete. I also enjoy snowboarding and windsurfing.

If not this profession, what would you have done?

If I had not been involved with hedge funds? I have always thought that being involved with wine and food would be something I enjoy. I wouldn't mind setting up a vineyard.

How do you see the investment industry in 10 years time?

That is a challenging time horizon for predictions in this fast-changing industry but I will give it a try. I believe that the specialisation and technical development of the industry will continue to grow rapidly. Derivative structures will continue to create more efficient markets and as such index and quant products will be more dominant, especially after a period of fee pressure that will squeeze the margins. Traditional asset management and hedge funds will morph together and the regulatory framework will make hedge fund investing more accessible and a mainstream investment. Aside from that, the hedge fund index business will have grown and will have established itself similarly to where indices on the traditional side are today. If hedge funds are seen as more traditional investment

---

4   We do note that we are talking about two different hypotheses of sustainable alpha creation and the ability to pick the right manager. Hypothesis #1 would be at the FoHF level, hypothesis #2 at the single-manager level. Indexing would offer a solution if hypothesis #1 ("can fund of funds create alpha?") would turn out to be false. Cloning could potentially offer a solution if both hypotheses turned out to be false (that is, there is no alpha generated at either the fund of fund or the single manager level). Again, the definition of alpha plays a major part, as clones assume 50% to 80% of claimed alpha to be beta.

products, we may see many more traditional products paired with hedge fund investments such as alpha-enhanced equity indices.

Finally – passive hedge fund investment: art, science or skill?

I would think all three. Science leads to the quantitative methods and robust technologies that form the foundation of our processes, and ensures unbiased representation of the index. It is also the basis for our tracking fund portfolio construction process. Skill is required to successfully employ these models. And art is drawn upon to ensure that the quantitative results make sense. If I had to lean towards only one of the three, I would say that the science of constructing a rules-based methodology for passive hedge fund investments and the management of quantitative index portfolios is the most important factor since it laid the groundwork for everything else.

Thank you for your time.

CONCLUSIONS

As to passive hedge fund investing, the cloning concept seems to be attracting the most interest at the moment, and may serve to put some pressure on hedge fund fees. We find the cloning concept very interesting, but we also acknowledge that there may be some more time needed to create a suitable track record, given the question mark on factor stability. Even if the factors are stable at present, the industry composition may change, and passive and active clones may show potential for more positive/negative surprises than a passive investor might be willing to accept. Furthermore, some of the active clones engage in distribution replication (that is, using forward-looking trading rules) rather than linear replication, even adding security selection. In this case, the clone is bordering on the fringe of global macro/multi-strategy managers possibly without regard to risk, return or beta considerations, while the fee levels are not too dissimilar. Nevertheless, cloning is the most liquid, transparent and low-cost alternative for beta investing into hedge funds.

On the other hand, there are products in the indexing space which track the broader aggregate rather than the investable indices using proxy managers, and with actual, rather than simulated, performance using tracking techniques from traditional asset classes. We note that these have delivered superior risk-adjusted performance to a number of FoHF, with higher liquidity and transparency. One of their drawbacks is that they do not avoid the second layer of fees, but rather minimise it. Their success will also depend on the available liquidity of the underlying managers, and there is also some academic debate as to whether a market portfolio of active managers would actually constitute a "market portfolio".

Both cloning and indexing offer a possible first step into passive hedge fund management, and potentially a core-satellite approach where only pure alpha is paid for, but one should be aware of the inherent constraints. At this stage the costs and constraints of obtaining beta through both cloning and indexation should still be weighed against the potential benefits, especially in less efficient asset classes such as hedge funds where there is still a somewhat higher dispersion and persistence of successful managers.

9. HOW PORTABLE IS HEDGE FUND SKILL?

An interview with Bruce Dresner and Paul
Bonde on alpha transport

*"I believe alpha transport represents a real paradigm shift
that is gaining momentum. In fact, we're likely just getting
started; perhaps we are at the end of the beginning."*
– Bruce Dresner

INTRODUCTION

Few long-only portfolio managers have been able to consistently
provide alpha over standard benchmarks. As a result, alpha transport (aka "portable alpha") has increasingly become a hot topic as
institutional investors look for new ways to boost investment returns.
Furthering the momentum is the growing availability of financial
instruments to easily separate alpha from beta, which frees investors to look for better sources of alpha. Alpha transport can be an
especially potent tool for investors with a large proportion of their
portfolios in more efficient markets.

When actually implementing a portable alpha program, investors
and their boards need to get comfortable with a number of issues:

- *The purity of the alpha engine may be a concern.* The selected alpha
  engine may have a beta or style bias. For instance, long/short
  investing often displays a small cap or value bias and the
  embedded stock leverage can amplify investor risks.

- *The correlation of the alpha engine with other parts of an investor's total
  portfolio may be a concern.* Not only is it important for an alpha
  engine to have low correlation to the beta of an alpha transport program, but it also should not add significantly to risks
  already present in other parts of the total portfolio.

- *Diversification within an alpha engine may be a concern.* Correlation between alpha sources should be low, and ideally not have a tendency to increase markedly in times of market stress.

- *It is not always easy or cost-effective to separate alpha from beta.* In some cases, alpha and beta are inextricably linked. It may be prohibitively costly, or even simply not possible, to use futures or other derivatives markets to remove unwanted beta exposure "attached to" attractive alpha sources.

- *Certain risks of an alpha transport program may be a concern.* Circuit breakers may result in suspension of futures trading and expose traders to market gaps. Swaps may eliminate basis risk and gap risk and involve limited recourse, but entail counter-party risk instead.

- *Liquidity issues may come into play.* Even where the beta exposure is attained through derivatives, cash may be required for deposits, margins, settlements, etc. Care must be exercised to ensure that cash is available when required, without incurring undue cost or disruption to the alpha sources.

Introducing our interviewees

Bruce Dresner

Since 2002, Bruce has been a Principal of BlackRock Alternative Advisors, a firm offering integrated financial services for private clients and institutions. He focuses on absolute return strategies with particular emphasis and portfolio management responsibilities relating to alpha transport strategies. Bruce also serves as a member of BlackRock Alternative Advisors' Investment Committee. Prior to joining BlackRock Alternative Advisors, he was VP for Investments and Chief Investment Officer at Columbia University. Before joining Columbia, he was Director of Investments and Chief Investment Officer at Dartmouth College. He was also the founding author of the annual National Association of College and University Business Officers ("NACUBO") Endowment Study. Bruce became a Chartered Financial Analyst charterholder in 1980. He received an MBA from the Amos Tuck School at Dartmouth College and a BA in Economics from the University of Miami.

Paul Bonde

Paul joined BlackRock Alternative Advisors in 2000 and is a Principal responsible for investment operations associated with the firm's alternative investments. Prior to joining BlackRock Alternative Advisors, he spent a total of nine years at Washington Mutual, Inc., coordinating the Corporate Internal Audit, Treasury Accounting and Corporate Accounting efforts. He also previously served as Director of Internal Audit at Great Northern Annuity, a subsidiary of GE Capital Corporation, and was a Senior Auditor with Price Waterhouse. Paul became a Chartered Financial Analyst charterholder in 2003. Additionally, he is a Certified Public Accountant (retired) and holds a BBA summa cum laude in Accounting from Pacific Lutheran University.

We will discuss the benefits and challenges of alpha transport with Bruce and Paul. Bruce will focus mainly on alpha sources and Paul on implementation nuances that institutional investors should consider.

Gentlemen, thank you for your time. Let's start with portable alpha – what sums up the concept?

BD: I feel that investors could think of alpha transport as an enhanced index strategy with a high probability of outperforming a long-only manager by a wide margin and with much greater consistency.

- It requires the investor to identify or assemble an alpha engine whose return stream has no more than a modest correlation to any of the primary markets.

- To generate performance above an investor's index benchmark (beta), the alpha engine must outperform the beta's cost of capital (3-month Libor plus a small spread, in most cases) and related expenses, such as management fees.

- In our experience, well-diversified low volatility hedge fund strategies give us the best opportunity to beat the hurdle on a consistent basis. The results so far have been very encouraging.

When and where did the concept originate?

BD: The alpha transport concept originated in the US and has been around for about 20 years. The strategy was originally popularised by a fixed-income investment company that realised: a) with a small amount of client capital it could obtain 100% exposure to the S&P 500 Index using futures; and b) it could apply its bond expertise to outperform the Libor rate (the cost embedded in the S&P 500 futures contact) by investing the remainder of the capital in short-term instruments that were a bit lower in quality and longer in duration. The long-term goal was to add 50bps to 100bps net of all associated costs annually. This enhanced cash alpha engine strategy works best when yield curves are upward sloping and spreads are wide, which is not the environment today.

What types of clients are currently embracing the portable alpha concept?

BD: I would say that a number of larger endowments were among the early adopters, but today alpha transport is gaining momentum among all different types of investors.

What are the constraints on portable alpha? (For example, regulatory or other.)

BD: I am not aware of any regulatory constraints. However, some clients have policy constraints that could keep them from embarking on a portable alpha program (such as restrictions on the use of derivatives). I believe the complexity of alpha transport has slowed its adoption, requiring "thinking outside the box". There are many good questions one can ask about alpha transport; the good thing is that investors can typically find equally satisfactory answers. Therefore, we feel that investors that take the time to learn about alpha transport strategies are likely to be well-rewarded over time.

How do clients manage the hidden beta exposure and the beta costs?

BD: One of the best ways to address concerns about hidden beta is through the proper identification or construction of an alpha engine. For example, alpha engines have often historically comprised short-duration fixed-income instruments or a diversified group of hedge funds because each would be expected to possess low correlation and modest beta to primary market risks, such as equity markets, interest rates, and currencies.

What are some of the more popular alpha/beta matches?

PB: Popular beta indices for US investors have included the S&P 500, the MSCI EAFE, the Lehman Brothers US Aggregate and the Russell 1000 and 2000. In theory, any index could be used as the beta component of an alpha transport program. However, beta costs are dependent, among other things, on the ability/willingness of the counterparty to hedge their side of the trade.

It is probably fair to say that much of the industry is still grappling with practical implementation issues. How does one obtain beta exposure? Could you compare futures versus swaps in terms of costs and benefits? Do clients usually prefer one over the other?

PB: We believe that gaining access to the respective beta index through the use of total return swaps versus futures is preferable for the following reasons:

- Futures contracts settle daily, requiring a cash reserve to satisfy margin calls. This creates a potential cash drag on performance.

- Futures are standardised products versus total return swaps, which can be customised.

BD: Of course, one of the counterarguments people often raise is that swaps entail counterparty risk. This is a valid concern, and is why one should work with counterparties that have strong balance sheets. However, it is equally important to note that in down markets, when one might expect counterparty risk to be greatest, the counterparty is owed a payment, not vice versa. The counterparty will owe a payment upon the swap's maturity in rising markets, when the counterparty's financial risk is likely a lesser concern. That should give investors an added measure of comfort. While it is an important component, I think it is fair to say that focusing too much on the beta is a bit of the tail wagging the dog. The dog is the alpha engine.

Can you comment a bit on rebalancing/transaction costs and cash flow management?

PB: The swap contracts usually have a maturity of one year. At the end of the one-year term, all amounts owed are net settled and paid. At that point, the contract can be rebalanced and rolled for another one-year term. By utilising one-year contracts with annual cash settlement, there is no need to retain a cash reserve. Instead, approximately 100% of the cash can be invested in the alpha engine on day one.

- The cost of the total return swap is the spread paid over the risk-free rate. For example, let's compare the S&P 500 to the Russell 2000. In an S&P 500 swap, the spread is currently positive (meaning the investor would pay a rate above the risk-free rate – usually 3-month Libor). In a swap referencing the Russell 2000, however, the spread is currently negative (meaning the investor would pay a rate below the risk-free rate). Thus, as you can see, the spread costs to the investor are dependent, in part, on the selected index.

- Spread costs are also impacted by the underlying collateral pledged in the transaction. For example, if Treasury securities were placed on deposit with the counterparty as collateral for a total return swap referencing the S&P 500, the spread would typically be in the 0 to 5bp range. If, however, shares in a fund of funds were pledged as collateral, the spread would increase. This is partly due to the fact that fund of hedge fund shares cannot be liquidated immediately to meet a margin call.

If we replace the Treasury securities as collateral from the client with an illiquid low-volatility fund of hedge funds like your own, how would this affect the annual cost?

PB: As mentioned above, pledging hedge fund shares as collateral will result in a higher spread than utilising very liquid instruments such as treasuries. That being said, BlackRock Alternative Advisors has spent a considerable amount of time educating counterparties about the fund of hedge funds alpha engine in order to increase their overall comfort level. As a result, the additional spread charged typically is very reasonable.

Additionally you mentioned that the spread on the Russell 2000 is negative; would this be a sign of the times? That is, people thinking small caps are overvalued at present? Would this be a potential technical sentiment indicator?

BD: There may be several reasons why one would be paid to go long the Russell 2000:

- It could be a sign of the times – in other words, investors are bearish on small caps, yet they do not want to liquidate their positions. So, they neutralise them by selling the Russell 2000.

- It could be that investors are finding small cap alpha, so they go long the manager and short the index, resulting in a pure alpha bet.

- It could be that people reduce transition costs by neutralising one manager and go into another through the overlay.

Whatever the reason, it is hard to draw any definite conclusions.

Are there any additional requirements you'd put on alpha to make it transportable?

BD: The transporting of the alpha is not the difficult part, although many people unfortunately spend way too much time focusing on that part. *The difficult part is generating alpha.* There are other desirable traits for the alpha source beyond modest beta and low correlation. You also want low volatility and consistently positive alpha. Because of this, I would think a number of hedge fund strategies are less suitable for an alpha engine:

- *Long/short equity:* may increase overall equity market risk if utilising an equity-oriented beta.

- *Illiquid alpha (such as private equity or real estate):* may not generate enough liquidity to pay the counterparty when required (such as when the market is down).

- *Global macro, directional strategies, or commodity-based strategies:* are volatile and unreliable in terms of alpha consistency, and often have a high attrition rate among managers.

Strategies that may serve as good alpha sources could include:

- market-neutral

- arbitrage

- special situations

- event-driven.

It is important to emphasise that for an alpha transport program to be successful, you don't need to be a hero. If you can get 200 to 300 basis points above Libor, that would be equivalent to a very high alpha for a long-only manager, probably top quartile or better. The concept of alpha transport is explained in figure 1.

Figure 1: The concept of portable alpha

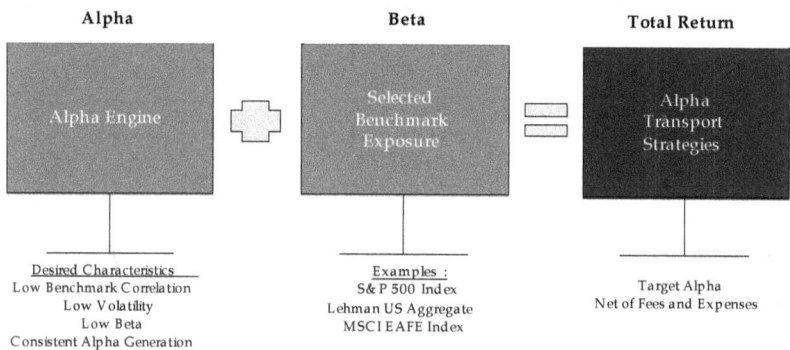

Source: BlackRock Alternative Advisors

Would a beta-to-beta swap make sense? For example, porting hedge fund beta (available through replication strategies) to traditional beta?

PB: In inefficient areas of investment, where better hedge fund managers tend to focus, knowledgeable investors should be able to outperform efforts that replicate average hedge fund performance. Therefore, this is an area where you probably do not want to accept the index return.

How do clients choose between allocating to alpha "attached to" asset classes represented within their strategic asset allocations and to portable alpha strategies?

BD: A positive aspect of an alpha transport strategy is that it doesn't need to impact stock or bond asset allocation decisions. Usually an investor is looking for an alternative to active management or passive/enhanced indexing because they want greater and more consistent outperformance. Typically, the by-product is also a better risk-adjusted return.

Let's talk about the role of hedge funds in alpha generation. Apart from low-volatility diversified funds of hedge funds, what single-manager single/multi-strategies would you consider useful as consistent transportable alpha sources?

BD: There are a lot of good single-strategy and multi-strategy managers out there. However, the issue is minimising the potential impact of Murphy's Law. Simply, diversification is an important element in risk management. Whether an investor builds a portfolio of hedge funds or uses a fund of funds, diversification increases the likelihood of achieving consistent alpha.

What are clients looking to optimise (apart from the information ratio)? For example, in terms of risk or other.

BD: The usual measures such as Sharpe and information ratio are quite valid. What alpha transport offers investors is the Holy Grail: bond-like risk with equity-like returns with no more than modest correlation. What surprises many is that alpha transport practitioners have been producing these types of results for a number of years. The proof is in the pudding. As a result, what was once considered an experiment has now become an acceptable technique.

On the other hand, I understand that people tend to have trepidation about entering alpha transport because it is more complicated. My suggestion would be for them to just dip their toe in the water. I'm sure their learning curve will increase exponentially. In the long run, we believe this effort will pay big dividends.

What would be the main risk to hedge funds as they are applied to alpha transport strategies? Is the total amount of alpha available to hedge funds falling?

BD: I would identify at least two risks, the first being a shock to the system. When such events occur, you will find that liquid positions will become more illiquid and correlations will increase. You don't want a negative beta to be compounded by negative alpha. So, one should worry about tail risk and lean toward a more conservative alpha engine.

The second is that alpha returns may well come down as more money and hedge fund managers enter the industry. This certainly seems to be a reasonable conclusion. Yet others feel that less-skilled managers represent an opportunity for those that are more skilled. The answer likely lies in between. Empirically, we have observed an increase in the number of skilled managers – such as from prop desks or the number two or three person at a hedge fund – going out and raising capital. The one thing you know for sure is that if hedge funds in aggregate are unable to outperform cash by a reasonable margin, they will all go out of business. We certainly are nowhere near that scenario.

It reminds me of what Mark Twain used to say: "Rumours of my demise are greatly exaggerated." With regard to alpha transport, I think 2% alpha is a reasonable and achievable minimum target for the foreseeable future, and 2% to 4% of alpha is a reasonable longer term objective.

Any other broader/investment issues you'd like to address?

BD: I believe alpha transport represents a real paradigm shift that is gaining momentum. In fact, we're likely just getting started; perhaps we are at the end of the beginning.

PB: I think one other interesting development is that we're starting to see more pension plans evaluating portable alpha products. Pension plans, for example, may have a long-term target return rate of 8% to 9% in order to meet their pension obligations. With US government bond yields in the 4% to 5% range, there seems to be greater focus on risk-adjusted returns and how a portable alpha product can positively add to returns.

What keeps you guys busy outside of office hours?

BD: I'm an investment junkie. Having said that, I enjoy spending time with family and friends, and also sit on the board of a foundation that in large part supports higher education, primarily the sciences and the arts (mainly the conservation of them).

PB: My wife would probably say I don't spend enough time outside of the office. When I am out of the office, in addition to spending time with friends and family, I enjoy volunteering and helping people understand basic financial skills such as budgeting, investing and saving money. Debt and a lack of savings by individuals are a growing problem in the US. I'd like to think we can solve this problem partly through better education.

Finally – investing in the future: art, skill or science?

BD: I've always felt the key to successful investing is the ability to adapt to change. Typically this also means focusing one's efforts on areas that are less travelled. So the more inefficient the asset class, the more art and skill is required.

PB: I agree wholeheartedly. It will never be a mechanical exercise. Investing, in a lot of cases, is more of an art and skill, especially in alternatives, and you'll see that in the wider dispersion of manager returns.

Thank you for your time.

Conclusion

The degree to which the characteristics mentioned may offset the benefit of an alpha transport strategy depends on the particular alpha and beta sources being considered. As such, it is important to carefully consider all factors, as well as the investor's liability structure, when developing the strategy.

However, as Bruce correctly points out, in many cases too much emphasis is put on the transactions which create the desired beta, which are mechanical and straightforward, whereas more attention should be put on getting the right market-neutral alpha engine.

As Bruce also mentions, alpha transport has a long history and the proof is in the pudding. For many clients the main hurdle will be education, and understanding the paradigm shift.

10. IS THE TREND STILL YOUR FRIEND?

An interview with David Winton Harding on
Commodities Trading Advisors

"Buy low, sell high. Fear ... that's the other guy's problem."
– Dan Aykroyd, in *Trading Places* (1983),
while cornering the orange juice futures market

AN INTRODUCTION TO COMMODITIES AND COMMODITIES TRADING ADVISERS (CTAS)[1]

As investors increasingly focus on the benefits of uncorrelated assets, commodities and managed futures funds are gaining more interest among institutional investors. In this section, we cover some of the considerations relating to CTA investment.

A landmark study on CTAs was presented way back in 1983.[2] The study concluded that returns from managed futures show surprisingly low correlations to those from stocks and bonds. Further research on more recent data suggests the following:

- CTAs performed well during the global liquidity crisis in 1998, as well as the global stock market decline from 2000 to 2003. CTAs show low to negative correlations to stock and bond returns, as during times of economic crises the prices of currencies and commodities tend to move in a volatile manner, creating profit opportunities.

---

1   CTAs or managed futures trade various instruments such as futures, forwards and options in over 150 different markets worldwide, generally using trend-following/momentum strategies.

2   As published in *The Potential Role of Managed Commodity Futures Accounts in Portfolios of Stocks and Bonds*, by Dr John Linter of Harvard University. Coincidentally, *Trading Places* hit the big screen in the same year.

- CTAs benefit from trending markets, but limit losses in sideways markets. Their nature is thus similar to a long call option on volatility. Examining the distribution of returns from the Barclays CTA index from 1985–2006, there is strong evidence that returns are positively skewed.

- Not only do CTAs display low correlation with traditional asset classes, they also show low correlation with other hedge fund strategies.

- Managed futures are highly transparent and liquid with daily exposure reports and position analysis being possible.

With global trends being more muted since 2004, and volatility lower, CTAs have started to experience difficulty in generating returns.

Although the CTA industry has grown at a rapid pace, the overall asset size has remained relatively modest.[3] Anecdotal evidence suggests that investors not familiar with CTAs tend to be concerned about the volatility. But the positive skew to returns mentioned above means that the most common volatility statistic (standard deviation) tends to overstate risk for CTAs, as the upside deviation tends to be more than twice the downside deviation. Historically, the emphasis has been on price-related factors using relatively simple but robust long-term trend-following systems (which critics say can be easily replicated). More recently, managers have been exploring additional factors, such as fundamental factors, the use of countertrend systems, dynamic capital allocation and pattern trading on different timeframes.

Introducing David Winton Harding

David Harding is one of the pioneers of trend-following systematic trading in the UK. Winton Capital Management Limited ("Winton"), which he founded in 1997, is now the third-largest CTA in the world with assets under management of $9.5 billion.

David began his career in the financial industry in 1982 after graduating from Cambridge University with a First Class Honours degree in Natural Sciences specialising in Theoretical Physics.

---

3 The industry size is estimated at US$182 billion in terms of assets under management as of 2Q 2007, according to the Barclays Group.

In 1987, David formed Adam, Harding and Lueck Ltd ("AHL"), a computer-driven, research-based CTA. Within four years AHL had grown into the UK's largest CTA with more than $300 million under management. In 1989, ED&F Man PLC ("Man"), currently one of the largest distributors of futures funds internationally, acquired a 51% stake of AHL, purchasing the remainder in 1994. David remained with the Man group for a further two years, running Man Quantitative Research, an in-house advanced statistical research team.

David founded Winton in February 1997 with a commitment to long-term quality scientific research. Winton currently employs over 130 people, including 70 PhDs and Masters degrees at two specialist research campuses in Oxford and West London.

We will discuss with David some of the aspects of CTA investing.

David, thanks for your time. Lately, commodities have been getting a lot of interest from institutional investors from both the alpha and beta perspective. Can you comment on how you see client interest in this area? Is it mainly passive beta futures or is demand for CTAs starting to take over?

Even though we're called a CTA, we have not much to do with commodities, although we invest a small percentage of our fund in it. CTAs are interesting in that they are the only category of hedge funds which are regulated (by the Commodity Futures Trading Commission). We're not a "Johnny come lately" to this business. I mean, we're not investing in commodities because some guru (like Jim Rogers) has become 10-year bullish on the asset class. And I hope our clients don't buy Winton because of its association with commodities. It's entirely coincidental.

Any crystal ball gazing on the long-term outlook for commodities?

It's best not to have a view on commodities, whether up or down. I'm fairly sceptical about the current interest from Wall Street. It's all about sales with lots of fees. Institutions are late to the game as usual. Whether oil is in contango is irrelevant. Markets are always changing. Some things do have persistence though, such as patterns in volatility, correlations.

Let's focus on some of your own work. What attracted you to commodities and CTAs in the first place?

The futures market is a very pure environment to test the EMH. You can go short and long with low transaction costs and implement refined statistics. If you want an environment to disprove the EMH, this is it.

Can you expand on what you see as the advantages and disadvantages of CTAs versus other hedge fund strategies?

I don't have a view on this, mainly because I don't understand many of the other hedge fund strategies. We are what we are. I don't know how many other hedge fund strategies are out there. But one thing I do know is that I don't agree with the whole alpha–beta concept.

There's this thing called beta, which is a market return, the return for a trading system that ranks stocks by market cap and has some rules for adding and deleting stocks. It has been proven to work, so it's not a useless trading system. Alpha is any other trading system's results compared to this trading system, and preferably uncorrelated. There are lots of layered concepts in there.

With the alpha–beta concept, I think the building has lost touch with the ground. Assets have expected returns and a covariance matrix. Managers try to forecast these two things to improve your portfolio. Even if you look at the stock index, what are the implied forecast covariances and expected returns?

Orthodoxy is the enemy of the mind. As Keynes used to say: "Practical men who believe themselves to be quite exempt from any intellectual influences are usually the slaves of some defunct economist." I don't know much about conventional portfolio theory but I'm sceptical about certain aspects of it. In many ways, our industry has more to do with compensation and marketing than it has to do with investment.

CTA returns seem to be less than what they used to be (for example, according to the Barclays CTA index).

Apart from the decline in volatility and lower leverage, what do you believe to be driving this outcome?

Be very sceptical when looking at indices. Most of these indices have not generated anything better than t-bills. I can say that both AHL and Winton have continued to generate good returns. A good fund manager by definition stands *against* the crowd. Hedge fund indexing went from zero to a big business. At some stage many lost money on a certain hedge fund index too.

The thing is, if this is an absolute return industry, then why should one compare it to indices at all? You're trying to make money. By the way, I am standing up for us as a company. I am not sure if I should stand up for the industry as a whole. I'm sure there are good honest companies out there. But many times, even for the big firms, I don't know what's going on inside.

CTAs frequently add new strategies to their core long-term trend-following programs; for example, pattern trading and mean reversion. How do you see CTA techniques developing to stay ahead of the curve?

We're very aggressive on R&D and spending a lot of money on all the things you listed. It's particularly striking how long trend-following has lasted. Perhaps people are indeed herding like social animals, and the financial CAPM followers may have to admit that people are not entirely rational indeed.

One argument that is in vogue at the moment is that as more and more CTAs add "fundamental" or "mean reversion to intrinsic value" analysis to their trading strategies, the line with, for example, global macro players becomes increasingly blurred.

I think we never aspired to be called anything. Many of the differences are mainly cosmetic and marketing. People are always limited by conventionalism. By changing the name you suddenly change the product. For example, institutions have been very accepting of GTAA players, but much less so of CTAs; we've only had increasing demand over the last two to three years.

Could you compare and contrast for us the pros and cons of discretionary versus systematic trading? Which do you prefer in general?

They are the same. Even for our systematic program, the computer is still being programmed by statisticians. Whatever the statisticians inferred was discretionary; that is, what will you research? When will you do it? It's a bit of an artificial distinction. Most people are locked in on the two extremes. Building a system requires a great deal of discretion as it is. There are projects, twists, and the system is constantly changing. Whatever it is though, it's not about reading the news and forming views.

What kind of returns can people reasonably expect from trend-following going forward?

It's probably more useful to talk about Sharpe ratios than absolute returns, as these would depend on the volatility taken. In general, one could expect a 0.75 Sharpe from CTAs.

Does a robust system necessarily have to be simple (or should it be complex)?

The more complexity, of course, implies more danger of self-delusion. Some complexity may add value. In general, simplicity in itself is not a good thing.

What do you think of some of the observations in the industry that most CTA returns can be passively replicated?

Well, good luck to them. About these passive replicators, let them try for 10 years or 20 years, or as long as we've been in business. I can tell you this: it's extremely hard work.

I think replicators represent a very complicated way of saying that we don't have any skills. Why, I can't believe there can still be business school professors who would argue that I have no skill. They have for a long time argued that Warren Buffett has no skill (or George Soros, or Jim Simons for that matter). They're corrupting young minds, and public money is actually spent to employ them.

Similarly, be very wary of what people on Wall Street and the hedge fund industry are telling you, and always keep an eye on your pockets.

What distinguishes a good from a poor CTA?

You could probably substitute "investment manager" for "CTA". I would say humility, patience, skill and intellectual curiosity. You should be doing it for the love of the game. As an investor, you should not get involved with "somebody who wants to make tons of money". These tons are usually for themselves, using other people's money. You know what they say about stockbrokers. They will manage your money, and manage it well, until it's all gone.

Could you compare and contrast the pros and cons of using a single CTA manager versus a fund of CTA funds? Has there been an increase in funds of CTA funds? Would the high correlation between trend-followers be a hurdle?

CTA funds of funds have been tried for over 20 years and haven't been very successful. You see, the non-offsetting of fees is a big issue. Also, what do you do when one CTA is long and one is short an overlapping position? You get double the management fee, performance fee and slippage, but end up with zero exposure. As to the correlations, that would be taken care of by proper portfolio construction.

For funds of hedge funds, how much should they allocate to CTAs?

They're pretty keen on CTAs now, especially after the 2003 bear market. Usually they pop up some quantitative model saying like: it should be 11.278% of their fund, or something like that. Whatever floats your boat. I am not a big believer in those allocation models.

What are your thoughts on the use of leverage by CTAs?

The lack of understanding of leverage is regrettable. Some investors come to me and say: you're a CTA, you're very risky. The point is that our system can handle any level of volatility, and that the leverage we operate with has been a business decision.

However, volatility can be tailor-made for any client. The more clever clients ask us about the Sharpe ratios. I would say over the last 50 years traditional stock markets have delivered Sharpe ratios of 0.2 to 0.3. Then why not invest 1% of your portfolio into something that will perform at a Sharpe of 0.75 or better?

Are there any indicators investors should watch out for when investing in CTAs?

Having a long track record definitely helps; also look at the drawdowns and find somebody with reasonably steady returns. Definitely know the references. There are an awful lot of crooks out there, and they always reappear. They will find new ways to find a new bunch of sheep to slaughter. The same thing happens every time.

If not this, then what would you be doing? What keeps you ticking?

I don't really know – I've never done anything else. I've got a young family, so I guess looking after small children would qualify. I enjoy reading and walking. There are so many good things out there, such as gardening, but I don't have the energy to apply myself seriously to any of them yet.

Finally – investing in the future: art, science or skill?

At Winton, we say it's about proper science applied to questions pertaining to investment. To make the distinction between the two is unhealthy. People always like to look at things in a binary fashion. If you understand statistics, you'd know there are many more things between 0 and 1.

It is true, though, that in the sixties investing was more of an art. In fact, you'd be likely to have a degree in history or such. Today, with all the available computing power, it's leaning more towards science.

CONCLUSIONS

CTAs remain one of the less understood strategies. They could fit in well with a focus on low correlation and capital preservation. And although it may seem counterintuitive, adding volatile managed futures funds could potentially reduce the overall risk of investment portfolios due to the negative correlation and positive skew (the "long call option" effect).

The unorthodox way that David views many things, including the alpha–beta and the portfolio construction discussion, was very refreshing. As David points out, the futures market is a very pure environment to test the EMH. You can go short and long with low transaction costs and implement refined statistics. If you want an environment to disprove the EMH, futures is it.

According to David, many of the differences between the more advanced CTAs and GTAA players are nowadays mainly cosmetic and marketing. Institutions have been very accepting of GTAA players for a long time, but much less so of CTAs, with institutional demand for CTAs only increasing over the last two to three years. It will be fascinating to see if interest in the two will merge over time.

PART VI:
ETHICAL INVESTING

11. ALPHA IN SUSTAINABLE INVESTING

An interview with Professor Rob Bauer on
optimising social and investment objectives

"That which is common to the greatest number has the least care bestowed upon it. Every one thinks chiefly of his own, hardly at all of the common interest; and only when he himself is concerned as an individual."
– Aristotle (384 BC–322 BC)

INTRODUCTION

In former times, there was a widely held view that institutional investors who want to do well may need to make a trade-off between investment performance and a social mission. Thinking on this issue seems to be changing.[1] Indeed, scandals like Enron or Worldcom have highlighted the high cost of unethical behaviour. For this chapter, we will examine the other side of the coin: does doing the right thing boost shareholder value? We will examine the different environmental, social and governance (ESG) factors that may impact companies and their valuations, and also examine sustainability investing from the firm (or micro) perspective, as well as the broader climate change (or macro) perspective. We will examine what academic literature and empirical evidence has to offer on how to best combine social and investment objectives.

---

1 According to Mercer's 2005 survey of 183 investment managers, 75% of US institutional investors recently polled believe that incorporating environmental, social or governance factors can be material to investment performance. And 60% believe an SRI approach will reduce risk or improve returns. As analysts continue to build models to incorporate material ESG factors into valuations and alpha forecasts, the trade-off between investment return and social return diminishes.

The micro perspective

Responsible investment may be defined as: *"Investment where social, environmental or ethical considerations are taken into account in the selection, retention and realization of investment, and the responsible use of rights (such as voting rights) attaching to investments."*[2]

At the risk of overgeneralising, three generations of socially responsible investing may be classified as follows:

- *First generation SRI* is based on moral or ethical beliefs and is driven primarily by faith-based and mission-based institutions. *Negative screens* are used to restrict investment in "sin stocks"; that is, firms involved in activities judged to be unacceptable. While different investors have different lists of "sin stocks", they commonly include firms involved in manufacturing or promoting alcohol, tobacco, adult entertainment, gambling and firearms. Negative screening continues to account for the majority of SRI assets.

- *Second generation SRI* involves the use of *positive screens*, seeking out companies whose social and environmental standards stand out among industry peers. Shareholder advocacy is a key element with the adoption of SRI proxy-voting guidelines, filing shareholder resolutions and engaging in dialogue with companies to promote social and environmental responsibility.

- *Third generation SRI* differs from second generation in that there is an explicit objective to use ESG factors to generate excess returns. Third-generation strategies represent a minority of SRI assets today, but there is a growing consensus that corporate social performance can impact stock prices and that sensitive management of ESG issues is simply good business. The term "sustainability" has become associated with this view and approach.

As sell-side research providers – such as Goldman Sachs, UBS and Citigroup – establish dedicated ESG research units, the nature of SRI research itself is changing. The next generation of research seeks to *measure* and *quantify* the effects of a company's management of environmental, social and governance issues.

---

2 Source: Mansley, M, 2000. *Socially Responsible Investment: A Guide for Pension Funds and Institutional Investors*, Monitor Press.

The macro perspective – climate change

Over recent years, climate change has become the focus of enormous public attention and emerged as a major political issue in many parts of the world. Climate change represents just one of a large number of ESG issues. It is, however, the issue which has caused many previous sceptics to rethink their approach to ESG.

In February 2007, the United Nations' Intergovernmental Panel on Climate Change released in Paris its most authoritative work on climate change, as the culmination of the work of 2500 scientists over six years.

- It details six scenarios under which temperatures are predicted to rise by at least 1.1 degrees and possibly as much as 6.4 degrees by 2100.

- The report concludes it is 90% likely that human activities led by burning fossil fuels account for most of the warming in the past 50 years.

- The report predicts rising sea levels, by 18 to 59 centimetres by 2100.

The steps governments are using to counter the effects of global warming include:

- emissions trading[3]

- nuclear power

- experimental technology such as clean coal[4]

- carbon sequestration[5]

---

3 Emissions trading: a limit or cap on the amount of a pollutant that can be emitted is set by governments. Companies or other groups that emit the pollutant are given credits which represent the right to emit a specific amount. The total amount of credits cannot exceed the cap. Companies that pollute beyond their allowances must buy credits from those who pollute less or otherwise generate excess credits.

4 Clean coal: the burning of coal is believed to be one of the principal causes of climate change. At this stage the process is theoretical and involves coal being chemically washed of minerals and impurities.

5 Carbon sequestration refers to processes that remove carbon from the atmosphere. A carbon dioxide (CO_2) sink is a carbon reservoir that is increasing in size, and is the opposite of a carbon "source". The main natural sinks are the oceans and plants and other organisms that use photosynthesis.

- ratification of the Kyoto Protocol[6]

- stimulate the use of renewable energy (such as wind, solar, hydro).

We will discuss sustainability investing and its ramifications for investors from the social and investment perspective with one of the leading experts in the field, Professor Rob Bauer, whereby we will examine both the micro and macro issues.

Introducing Rob Bauer

Rob Bauer is a Professor of Finance (chair: Institutional Investors) at Maastricht University in the Netherlands and an adviser to the board of ABP Investments. In addition, he is a senior researcher of Netspar and board member of the International Centre for Pension Management at the Rotman Business School in Toronto. He is also a member of the board of the postgraduate course on investments at the Free University of Amsterdam, and teaches various executive courses, among others IIR, TIAS, AIF, and the Dutch Financial Analysts Association (VBA). His present research focus is on ESG investments (SRI), corporate governance, asset liability management, risk budgeting, and stock selection. Rob's research has won him the Moskowitz Prize (in 2002 and 2005) for best quantitative study in the SRI domain, and the European Finance & Sustainability Research Award.

Rob, let's talk about socially responsible investing. To start off with, the UN's Principles of Responsible Investment[7]: what do they mean to you?

I think it's a reflection of the fact that many parties are now actually starting to take things seriously and responsible investing is

---

6 The Kyoto Protocol (1997) assigns mandatory targets for the reduction of greenhouse gas emissions to signatory nations. As of December 2006, a total of 169 countries and other governmental entities have ratified the agreement.

7 The UN Principles for Responsible Investment (PRI) launched in April 2006 is a voluntary code for investors aimed at raising awareness of corporate and environmental responsibility. At that time 50 institutional investors representing more than US$4 trillion in assets pledged support. As of May 2007, there are more than 187 signatories representing US$8 trillion. Mercer was consultant to the United Nations through the development of the Principles for Responsible Investment.

finally becoming mainstream. In the old days responsible investing received a lot of negative feedback from people who didn't believe in it. As an adviser within the investment community, I think it's a very good start. Of course, you can interpret it in many ways, from a little voting to having an integrated approach.

Can you compare and contrast for our readers how you see the difference between SRI and ESG? Is there any?

I get this question a lot. The way I see it, ESG provides the information that you can use for investing; it is all about the micro-economic content. SRI more reflects the way you put together a portfolio.

You recently started the European Centre for Corporate Engagement (ECCE) as a research platform.[8] Could you tell our readers a bit more about this initiative and what its objectives are?

At ECCE we try to focus on three things:

- *Content:* we try to fill the academic gap that we think exists on ESG literature, by linking ESG to firms, and investor portfolios. As researchers, we can be objective; that is, we have no vested interests in, for example, not publishing any negative findings.

- *Dialogue:* we discuss with analysts how this information is best used. If nobody is using it, then how can it be priced in?

- *Engagement:* we try to measure all the activism that is going on and try to see whether it makes sense. A problem is that a lot of this information is proprietary and can be seen as a source of competitive advantage, and hence may not be easily disclosed.

We try to expand our research to corporate finance and accounting too. The research topics can be quite broad. For example, we

---

8   ECCE is a joint initiative of Professor Kees Koedijk, affiliated with the Erasmus University/Rotterdam School of Management, Professor Rob Bauer of the University of Maastricht, and assistant professor Jeroen Derwall. In 2002 and 2005, their team received the US Social Investment Forum's prestigious Moskowitz Prize. Also in 2005, they obtained a large grant from the Swedish Foundation for Strategic Environmental Research (Mistra) to conduct research into the role of financial markets in promoting sustainable development. These awards have underpinned the existence of the ECCE. International ties have been established with Governance Metrics International (GMI) and Innovest Strategic Value Advisors, among others.

recently examined the impact of ESG on European corporate bond yields and credit default swaps. One would think that if money is spent on ESG, bondholders might see that as a cash outflow. It turned out that they saw it as a sign of a more healthy company, so it was priced in positively.

What are some of the main barriers to responsible investing? For example, the benefits are often intangible or can't be measured.

I think some of the barriers include the fact that it's often not clear what we're talking about and also that there can be a lot of conflict of interest in the financial sector.

This can be on a macro level. For example, let's say Philips doesn't like Sony for some ethical issues – if Philips makes this clear, Sony might strike back with something else they have on Philips. So there is a natural incentive for firms not to ask each other about it.

On a micro level, a portfolio manager may not want to be restricted in his investment universe as this will affect his financial reward (the bonus schemes) at the end of the year.

To what extent is the traditional SRI investor base shifting, along with perceptions of SRI, and why?

The key thing is that SRI is going mainstream, and there is more and more participation from the public. Somebody once said to me that he estimates 1% to 2% of mandates fall under the SRI niche. I would guess that perhaps over 20% of investors may be somehow integrating SRI into their investment process and policies in one way or another.

How do you see SRI going forward? Do you support the "integrated view"?[9]

I fully support the integrated view. There are issues that make sense; for example, 80% of how successful a company will be may depend on how innovative it is. ESG can help you pick those successful companies.

---

9   As mentioned before, the three approaches prevalent in SRI are: 1) the use of negative screens (excluding certain sectors such as drugs and tobacco); 2) the use of positive screens (best in class); 3) the integrated approach, combining sustainability with financial research throughout the process.

Can you comment on any recent academic research linking company valuations to "doing the right thing" (especially quantitative research)? You might like to talk about some of your own findings and perhaps discuss the concept of eco-efficiency.[10]

Well, in essence there are three competing hypotheses:

1) *Extra-financial information is relevant.* We did some research (*Financial Analysts Journal*, 2005) and we found that eco-efficiency and high corporate governance did confirm hypothesis 1.

2) *Extra-financial information is not relevant.* There are also studies on SRI mutual funds (including one of my own!) that show no differences relative to conventional funds.

3) *Extra-financial information is relevant, but in a negative manner.* There are articles that mention that there is a "price for sin". That is, there is an extra return for the risk premiums you run for investing in, for example, defence and tobacco stocks.

To make things confusing, you can actually find academic evidence for all three hypotheses. At ECCE we try to broaden the research on these hypotheses, and focus on not only the management but also the financial implications.

You're probably familiar with the so-called basic law of active management: a reduced opportunity set in terms of the number of available stocks leads to a lower information ratio.[11] **What does empirical evidence show in terms of alpha generation by SRI investors as they invest in a reduced universe?**[12]

---

10 For example, Guenster, N, Derwall, J, Bauer, R, and K Koedijk. "The economic value of corporate eco-efficiency." Working Paper, Erasmus University, 25 July 2005. This study won the 2005 Moskowitz Prize for the best quantitative study of socially responsible investing. Broadly, we can define eco-efficiency as creating more value with fewer environmental resources, resulting in less environmental impact (for example, less pollution or natural resource exhaustion).

11 Grinhold and Kahn, 2000, *Active Portfolio Management*, Irwin.

12 For example, Derwall et al. (2005) find eco-efficient companies to have better returns. On the other hand, Hamilton (1993) and Bauer (2005) seem to find similar returns for SRI and conventional funds. Milevsky et al. (2006) find that eliminating a small number of "undesirable" stocks seems to have no significant economic penalty on maintaining a passive index. Also, sin industries seem to do well (for example, the US Vice Fund which invests in gambling, tobacco and defence has done exceptionally well).

The basic law is true. But even in a reduced opportunity set, you can find stocks that mimic other stocks in such a way that you do not lose much in the way of added value. Of course, only buying a few ethical stocks or just applying negative screening will get you into trouble. But then again, isn't any portfolio a restricted number (or subset)? Then, why not buy ESG companies that may perform better?

Rob, let's discuss climate change – this issue seems to be "front and square" in the minds of many investors, and the public for that matter. Critics of Kyoto argue that China, India, and other developing countries will soon be the top contributors to greenhouse gases.[13] Without Kyoto restrictions on these countries, industries in developed countries will be driven towards these non-restricted countries, thus there is no net reduction in carbon. What do you think of this?

I'm not really a climate change expert, but it does seem clear to me that on a number of issues we need globalisation; that is, to really integrate ESG on a large scale, we need rules that are enforced for everyone.

Turning to the climate capitalist in all of us, how can investors benefit from climate change? For example, investing in clean energy[14] /carbon sequestration (forests, etc.) or the carbon credit market?[15]

I think clean energy (venture capital) is very innovative and interesting. As to the carbon credit market, things have improved, as big investors are now involved. All this has made the price of carbon more transparent. Of course, there are many more ideas; for example, you may want to consider investing in firms that spend a higher proportion on R&D in this field.

---

13 The United States and Australia have not joined Kyoto. Other countries, such as India and China, which have ratified the protocol, are not required to reduce carbon emissions under the present agreement despite their relatively large populations.

14 Investment in the cleantech sector has grown from a mere $7 billion in 1995 to $30 billion in 2004 and a record $63 billion in 2006. It is projected that annual growth will be between 20% and 30% per year for the next decade.

15 Around two years old, estimated at $22 billion as of end of 2006.

What risks does climate change pose to investors, and over what time horizon? How are investors working to manage these risks?

Well, you probably would like to distinguish between long-term investors such as pension funds and insurance companies and short-term companies such as hedge funds. For long-term investors, it may lead to poor returns in the long run. There will be higher uncertainty, which will increase the discount rate in the long run.

For short-term investors, if prices have not reflected all this, you might want to take advantage of this. For example, there are more and more hedge funds emerging with an SRI theme.

If we think about investor education, right now you can do an MBA and CFA and not learn how to value environmental externalities. How and when will this change? Does it need to?

I think this is changing. It's already an elective in a number of courses. Of course you could study it as a full degree, but then where do you find a job (until it becomes more mainstream)? I think the CFA by the way does do research on it. There were some documents and surveys done on it, and I wouldn't be surprised if it makes it into the curriculum soon.

One could possibly argue that population growth has been the main driver behind climate change, the peak in oil supply and the water shortage in some countries (such as Australia). In the 60 years since World War II, the world population has grown at an unprecedented rate, from 2.5 billion to 6.5 billion today, with 9 billion forecast by 2050.[16] Of these, 8 billion will be in developing countries, with over 5 billion city-dwellers, and 25% of the population retired. That's a lot of shocks to the system. What's your long-term "world vision" and its effect on natural resources?

I'm not a futurist, but let me tell you about the situation in the Netherlands, a pretty small country. Right now we've got 7 million cars. This is expected to reach 12 million in 2025, so it's clear that

---

16 Based on Societe Generale, "The challenges facing the world economy", May 2007.

we've got a total disaster on our hands. What we desperately need is some vision and innovation. We need to take away the barriers to innovation.

How do you see the effects of your "world vision" impacting the investment industry in 10 years time? And 50 years time?

It's already impacting the investment industry. Analysts are always on the lookout for innovation and new ratios to analyse. We'll probably reach a point where all of a firm's expected ESG innovation will be discounted into the prices, at which stage only unexpected changes will matter.

In general, how do you rate the progress that has been made in the sustainability/ESG area this decade?

I would say investors over the past decade have focused mainly on the governance bit, with lots of shareholder engagement. The attention given to the E&S part has been very scarce until, say, two to three years ago. Now that the mainstreaming is coming about, I expect more progress in these areas. Again, I think the UN PRI have been very beneficial to the industry as a whole.

Are there any differences across regions in the rate of progress and, if so, what have been the key influences behind them?

Well, I recently went to Japan and I would say that pension funds over there are not embracing the concept as yet. It probably has something to do with their cultural background. I'd say Europe is leading the way and also Canada. Traditionally in Europe there has been more focus on the needs of the different stakeholders. In the US many times the agency costs act as barriers.

What keeps you busy outside of office hours?

(Laughs.) That would be my three little boys and the soccer team they play in (I coach the junior soccer team). I also play tennis. I have to admit I find it a bit of a challenge to be as socially responsible as I would ask from a company. I know many times I should have walked instead of taking the car, etc. It's something I struggle with.

Finally – sustainability investment/ESG analysis/ socially responsible investing/responsible investing: what should it be called?

Sustainable investing is the best term. The confusion about the definitions is certainly not helping the discussions.

Thank you for your time.

CONCLUSIONS

For many companies the focus on the short term is damaging to long-term business prospects. Although they are often aware of issues which have potential to affect their businesses over the long term, and of ways to address them, they are reluctant to take action if there will be a short term "hit" to earnings. This is because they do not think that shareholders are themselves sufficiently focused on the long term. However, for companies there will be increased competitive, regulatory and reputation risk as they continue to shy away from taking action. And we believe that a growing number of institutional investors truly require their investee companies to take a broader approach to business and risk management, encompassing sustainability principles.

Similarly, the investment management industry may be forced to integrate sustainability issues into the investment process and accept a longer term focus. The institutions which have adopted the UN Principles of Responsible Investing are a major force in the market and will increasingly be assessing managers according to their alignment with the principles.

Part VII: Beyond the Ivory Tower

12. WHAT'S NEW IN MODERN FINANCE?

An interview with Professor Stephen Brown
on developments in modern finance

"Prediction is very difficult, especially if it's about the future."
– Niels Bohr (1885–1962)

MODERN FINANCE REVISITED

Many decades before the development of what is now known as modern finance, there was interest in technical analysis, as well as early versions of the random walk hypothesis. For instance, the Dow theory was first documented in 1882, and as far back as 1900 Louis Bachelier noted: "The mathematical expectation of the speculator is zero." However, Markowitz's work on modern portfolio theory (MPT) in 1952 and Sharpe's introduction of capital asset pricing theory (1964) are widely regarded as representing the beginning of the transformation of investment management from an art to a science.[1] Trading on intuition and a feel for the market was over time replaced by an emphasis on risk-adjusted returns, correlations, and diversification.

A further major landmark work was the development of the efficient markets hypothesis (EMH) as presented by Eugene Fama (1970). Post 1970, modern finance has dominated the financial economics literature, with the EMH achieving enormous profile during the 1970s and beyond. Fama referred to three forms of market efficiency. The implication of the strongest form of the EMH is that

---

1 Although Markowitz's work can be credited with eventually leading to much greater rigour in investment management, he suggested that the key to forecasting might be found in a mixture of "statistical techniques" and "the judgment of practical men". In essence, even Markowitz acknowledged that anticipating the future can be as much an art as a science.

it is almost impossible to beat the market. Of course, in any year active managers' returns are distributed around the overall market returns and some managers are ahead of the market. Proponents of the EMH argue that although every year about one-third of active fund managers beat the market, each year it is a different group with the make-up of the outperformers in any period being driven largely by luck.

More recent developments

A key assumption of the EMH relates to "homo economicus", the assumption that we all behave in a rational manner. Not too long after its introduction, evidence that markets may perhaps not be so efficient began to accumulate and anomalies began to emerge systematically. A small industry developed devoted to investigating the behaviour of markets, and the discovery and documentation of a number of anomalies seemed to refute the idea that market prices incorporate all information rationally and instantaneously. Examples were the tendency for value stocks to outperform growth stocks and small caps to outperform large caps. Fama[2] himself authored and co-authored a number of articles during the 1970s advancing a number of possible explanations for the observed outperformance of value stocks, the favoured one being that they are more risky.

Behavioural finance, or the ability to profit from other investors' mistakes, subsequently emerged as one of the more intricate and controversial topics in modern finance and as a significant challenge to the notion of market efficiency. For example, a landmark work on behavioural finance titled "Contrarian Investment, Extrapolation and Risk" was published by Josef Lakonishok, Andrei Shleifer and Robert Vishny in 1994 (this trio became known as LSV).[3]

LSV argue that value stocks are less risky than growth stocks, not more risky, and that their undervaluation represents but one of many anomalies which are exploitable due to repeating human

---

2 Eugene Fama is most often thought of as the father of the efficient market theory. Together with Kenneth French he produced the three-factor model of risk, attributing differences in stock returns to: 1) beta, 2) size, and 3) book-value-to-price ratio.

3 The key notion of the 1994 article is that investors tend to extrapolate past performance and tend to overpay for "glamour stocks", and underpay for "out of favour stocks". The authors eventually received the Roger F Murray Award for this paper.

behaviour. This proposition stands directly against the work of efficient market proponents such as Fama.[4]

Behavioural finance was for some time regarded as a collection of market anomalies that defy efficient markets, rather than being a coherent theory, although lately there have been attempts to bring it together into a more integrated framework. A number of investment management firms have been successfully built around the exploitation of market anomalies, mostly from the value side, even if their principals were not fully immersed in or even conscious of the academic debate.

In more recent times, leading academics such as Andrew Lo (2004) have introduced the *adaptive markets hypothesis*, working on theories of evolutionary dynamics and arguing that much of what behavioural finance cites as counterexamples to economic rationality – such as loss aversion, overconfidence, overreaction, mental accounting, and other behavioural biases – are, in fact, consistent with an evolutionary model of individuals adapting to a changing environment via simple heuristics.

Introducing Professor Stephen Brown

Stephen J Brown is David S Loeb Professor of Finance at the Leonard N Stern School of Business, New York University. He graduated from Melbourne High School and Monash University in Melbourne and studied at the University of Chicago, earning an MBA in 1974 and a PhD in 1976. Following successive appointments as a Member of Technical Staff at Bell Laboratories – where he spent time on assignment as District Manager in the AT&T Pension Fund – and Associate Professor at Yale University, he joined the faculty of New York University in 1986. In December 2002 he was appointed to the honorary position of Professorial Fellow with the title of Professor at Melbourne Business School of the University of Melbourne.

He has served as President of the Western Finance Association and Secretary/Treasurer of that organisation, has served on the Board of Directors of the American Finance Association, and was one of the founding editors of the *Review of Financial Studies*.

---

4 Both Lakonishok and Fama agree that a basket of value stocks will over the long run outperform a basket of growth stocks, though for different reasons.

He is one of the Managing Editors of *The Journal of Financial and Quantitative Analysis*, has served on the editorial board of *The Journal of Finance*, and is on the board of the *Pacific-Basin Finance Journal*. He has published numerous articles and four books on finance and economics-related subjects. He is currently retained as an adviser to MIR Investment Management Ltd in Sydney, and has served as an expert witness for the US Department of Justice. He is married and has two children.

We will discuss the current trends in modern finance with Professor Stephen Brown.

Stephen, many thanks for this interview. First, can you introduce our readers to what you consider to be the most interesting and fertile topics of discussion in modern finance today?

Most of the more interesting and fertile topics of discussion today have to do with the role of institutions within markets.

Risk research attracts attention. The simple-minded covariance-based definitions of risk have been effectively challenged by the development in the recent past of the hedge fund industry. This has spotlighted the importance of more nuanced measures of downside risk, tail risk and operational risk, which is my current area of interest and research. The same set of concerns has raised issues both in terms of the importance of systemic risk, and also in terms of corporate governance. This has reinvigorated interest and research on these topics.

Behavioural finance: Some of the original great promise of the behavioural view of the markets has been tempered somewhat by what I would term *the failure to generate a unified paradigm of asset pricing* through this analysis. Some of the emphasis in this literature has shifted away from the macro level question of how asset prices are determined to a more micro level understanding of the behaviour of corporate managers in setting corporate financial policy, and in terms of the behaviour of traders in real-time markets.

Some of the great questions of financial theory remain with us, in particular the way in which expected return relates to measures of risk. A celebrated paper by Lettau and Ludvigson[5] shows that

---

5   Martin Lettau and Sydney Ludvigson (2001), "Resurrecting the (C)CAPM: a cross-sectional test when risk premia are time-varying", *Journal of Political Economy*, v. 109 , pages 1238–1287.

the apparent disconnect between asset prices and the real economy, one of the principal arguments posited for the behavioural view of the markets, can be ascribed to the failure to control for the dynamic changes that have occurred within the markets over the last 50 years. Controlling for these factors does indeed explain the cross-sectional dispersion of expected returns relative to risk.

Which discussions are most likely to affect the way that institutional investors behave in the near future?

At least in the United States, *the first concern of most investment fiduciaries is risk management.* Paradoxically, *it is this concern that is leading many fiduciaries to hedge funds, not in the naive belief that hedge funds are in fact hedged, but rather as a tool for effective diversification.*

However, the failure of Amaranth Advisors last year was a wake-up call for many investors. The lack of transparency of most hedge funds is a source of considerable operational risk, and there is a considerable interest in devising more sophisticated measures of risk. Hedge funds are also an expensive way to obtain effective diversification, and this has lead recently to the growth of beta funds, passively managed vehicles that mimic the risk characteristics of hedge funds but without the high cost structures and operational risk features of typical hedge funds.

Do you want to comment on any interesting trends you see in the quantitative research field?[6]

This is very much a matter of taste. I am intrigued by what I am reading about the behaviour of individual investors from some of the large-scale databases in the United States and in Sweden, particularly in the work of Zoran Ivković and others.[7] *Contrary to the assumptions and predictions of modern portfolio theory, individual investors do not hold well-diversified portfolios and tend to invest in only the familiar.* While of course consistent with the behavioural hypothesis, this does tend to challenge the perceived wisdom on return for risk trade-offs, and

---

6 As noted above, Stephen also serves as Managing Editor of *The Journal of Financial and Quantitative Analysis.*

7 While this emerging literature is very large, the paper of Ivkovich, Z, Sialm, C, and SJ Weisbenner, "Portfolio concentration and the performance of individual investors", AFA 2006 Boston Meetings (available at SSRN: http://ssrn.com/abstract=568156) forthcoming in the *JFQA*, is a very good example.

has significant implications that might explain why there appears to be such a pronounced home bias in international investing.

Meanwhile the increased attention to institutions and markets in United States–based research is challenging some of the cherished examples cited in the behavioural literature. The discount at which closed-end funds trade relative to the value of assets under management is often presented as an unexplained anomaly, or rather as evidence for a behavioural view of the markets. Stephen Ross at MIT argues that this and many other so-called anomalies arise out of an incomplete understanding of the institutional features and tax regimes much overlooked by US-based researchers. His recent book is a must-read.[8]

Many former academics have left the ivory tower to pursue active careers in fund management; for example, Josef Lakonishok (LSV), Richard Roll (Roll and Ross Asset Management), Jim Simons (Renaissance) and even Eugene Fama himself. You yourself are at present associated with MIR. What's your view on this:

  a) **In terms of what it implies for the EMH?**
  b) **Does book-smart win over street-smart?**
  c) **Does exposure to day-to-day funds management issues assist an academic in developing insights and ideas for further research?**

a) What it implies for the EMH:
Many in funds management see the role of academics as seekers after regularities in the market, regularities that are profitable. Given the faith that many academics seem to have in the efficient markets hypothesis, there is perceived to be some tension here between what they seem to believe in and what they aspire to do. Hence there is some scepticism of their role, a scepticism that is reflected in Roger Lowenstein's aptly titled book on the collapse of Long Term Capital Management, *When Genius Failed.* What can possibly be the role of these pointy-headed folks in the real work of funds management?

I am convinced that this characterisation of the role of academics is as much a straw man as is the representation of the efficient markets hypothesis they are said to believe in.

---

8 Ross, S, *Neoclassical Finance*, Princeton University Press, Princeton, 2004.

The academic perspective gives a useful reality check on exuberance, a hard-edged understanding of the trade-off of return for risk, and most of all, an important measure of humility both in terms of the history of the markets and the powerlessness of any individual to correct or stop general market movements. For me, this is what the EMH means. It is not a straw man view that it is impossible to make money trading. Rather, it is a dose of healthy scepticism. When you see a security that is trading considerably less than its intrinsic value, do you *buy* or ask *why*?

b) Does book-smart win over street-smart?
I am not of the view that there is a contest between "book-smart" and "street-smart". There is room for both. A qualitative seat-of-the-pants approach may lead to quick decisions but may lack discipline. Quantitative approaches, to use a phrase of my friend Michael Triguboff, are often blunt tools that attribute value to factors otherwise left out of the analysis. My funds management experience shows very clearly the value of a carefully mediated compromise between these approaches. And it is not a one-way street. Most of the important advances in academic research, in asset allocation, performance measurement and derivative pricing have arisen from observations of the markets and the curiosity and the need to explain regularities that are otherwise hard to understand. The very term "anomalies" refers to the fact that there are things that as academics we cannot explain and need to explain, and has been a large part of the motivation for the growth and development of the behavioural finance area.

However, there is a temptation to label everything we cannot understand as "behavioural". Burton Malkiel and Richard Quandt in 1969 wrote a book[9] in which the odd behaviour of option traders was discussed and the fact that they used a simple rule of thumb d*S − b*PV(exercise) to value options which gave valuations for out-of-the-money calls and puts that were too high and valuations for in-the-money options that were too low relative to the actuarial models of valuation then popular among academics. This formula was described in a doctoral dissertation at the University of Chicago in 1962 by James Boness, but it reflected current practice. This

---

9   *Strategies and Rational Decisions in the Securities Options Market*, MIT Press, Cambridge, 1969.

was therefore an anomaly. It was not until the work of Black and Scholes published in 1973 that we came to understand the rational basis of this formula.

Indeed, I believe that the major contribution of academics has been the growth and development of financial technology, exemplified by the option pricing model, a cornerstone of all new financial claims markets. Coincidently, these developments have been matched by computational innovations that have made these markets feasible. One unintended consequence of this technology has been to make redundant the old seat-of-the-pants trader. I discourage students from going into sales and trading as I foresee that many of the jobs in the field are being taken by cyber-traders, of the kind pioneered by Jim Simons at Renaissance Technologies, traders who don't sleep, who don't have temper tantrums and who never confuse buy and sell orders.

Beyond these very specific examples, academics can play a very important role in funds management by providing a fresh and sometimes completely different perspective. Academics are not driven by the imperative of devising ever new trading rules and searching out market opportunities. They are thus in a position to provide a reality check to fund managers who have data mined and backtested just one time too many.

c) Does exposure to day-to-day funds management issues assist academic research?

In a real sense, I have been associated with fund management since I left graduate school in 1976, first at AT&T's Pension Fund, then at Yamaichi Securities in Tokyo and now at MIR.

Fund management can provide the academic with significant benefits by assessing the practical limitations that confront the implementation of research ideas. We had a term for this at Bell Labs. It was referred to as "reduction to practice", a term from patent law that reflected the fashioning of pure research and indeed the research agenda to the practical limitations of implementation. Every one of the Nobel Prize winners at Bell Labs had done first-rate pure research with path-breaking practical implications. Even Arno Penzias who discovered the echo of the Big Bang (for which he won the Nobel) was chiefly interested in the application of this research to the particular problems of reducing interference in long distance radio telephony.

Dr Penzias as President of Bell Labs came into my office once and challenged me to explain the possible benefits of my well-cited research on event studies, the empirical analysis of information events on stock prices. How could this research have any possible benefit to the telephone company? I asked him whether he participated in AT&T's $35 billion superannuation fund. Did he know that there was very little understood about the statistical properties of measures used to assess the performance of the 108 manager mandates? I then laid out for him the close, indeed intimate relationship between my academic research and matters of the greatest practical concern for the company, questions that had motivated my research in the first place. This was exactly what he wanted to hear.

I notice that you co-authored an article on the Dow theory back in 1998, which concluded that the timing strategy actually yielded a positive alpha.[10] Can you outline for our readers your view on the EMH in its various forms?

Twenty years ago or so, the tobacco industry in the United States went on a publicity offensive arguing that because science could not attribute all lung cancer to smoking, it was okay to light up.

In the same way many fund management companies argue today that because the EMH does not explain all regularities in asset pricing, it is okay to engage in simple-minded market-timing strategies. It is all a question of degree and context. Yes, the data is indeed in conflict with the EMH in its various flavours and degrees. This does not mean that it is easy to make money in the markets. Sophisticated hedge funds in the city can make money from the regularities that academic research has found in the markets. People out in the country with full-time jobs outside the financial sector and lacking timely information may as well assume that the EMH is literally true.

---

10 Alfred Cowles' (1933) test of the Dow theory apparently provided strong evidence against the ability of Wall Street's most famous chartist to forecast the stock market. In Stephen's paper, he reviewed Cowles' evidence and found that it supports the contrary conclusion – that the Dow theory, as applied by its major practitioner, William Peter Hamilton, over the period 1902 to 1929, yielded positive risk-adjusted returns. A re-analysis of the Hamilton editorials suggests that his timing strategies yield high Sharpe ratios and positive alphas.

This point is illustrated by my research on the Dow theory. Many people believe they know what the Dow theory is, but in fact it was never written down by Charles Dow. All we know about this theory is what was written by his most earnest acolyte, William Peter Hamilton. And his writings were not altogether transparent. Many people believe that the Dow theory was simply a matter of observing head and shoulders formations in simple charts. But it was never that simple. My co-authors and I used advanced neural net procedures to capture the essence of the Dow theory from the writings of Hamilton given the market conditions of the time. We were able therefore to create a Hamilton automaton that survived his death. This automaton made money from the early thirties through the fifties, but then struggled as the markets became more sophisticated and the easy money filtered away. In context it was possible to yield positive alpha through this rather mechanical timing strategy, but not now, not in today's market conditions. Now of course, Hamilton and his mentor Charles Dow were very sophisticated analysts. In conducting this experiment, my co-authors were very tempted to allow the Hamilton automaton to live and to learn.

I am sure that Hamilton, were he to be living today, would find a way of profiting from the time series regularities in the market. But it would not be Dow's theory. Simple-minded mechanical black boxes that worked in the 1920s and 1930s cannot be expected to work in the much more sophisticated market conditions of today.

What's your view on behavioural finance? Does it work, and if so, is there any prospect that enough of us will be able to re-program ourselves so that it will stop working?

In the academic literature, there is much excitement about the potential of behavioural finance to explain many apparent and otherwise inexplicable regularities in the financial markets. The great challenge of this theory is to develop a unified or single theory which will coherently explain asset prices. At the moment, this body of work represents a series of ill-connected examples which severally explain certain market regularities. But as GK Chesterton wrote many years ago, 10 false philosophies will fit the universe. Many of these behavioural stories while plausible by themselves need to be shown to work together to explain asset prices. Many of the brightest people in the US are working to meet this challenge.

My good friend and mentor Stephen Ross of MIT presents a strong challenge to the behavioural literature in his recent book.[11] Just because we as academics are not able to explain a particular regularity in the markets does not make it irrational or "behavioural". Perhaps we need to work just a little harder?

In the funds management area behavioural finance is a Siren call that can bring many on to the rocks. The academic literature is very convincing. It does work. But it is dangerous to try to make money from it for we must necessarily assume that the fund manager is immune from the behavioural biases that infect everyone else. It is therefore self-defeating in practice.

In Homer's epic, Odysseus understands that to listen to the Sirens is to drive his boat on to the rocks on which they sit. He therefore commanded his crew to tie him to the mast and to put wax in their ears. He was entranced by the call of the Sirens and called on his crew to steer the boat toward them. But they did not hear him and he sailed to safety. The only effective way to profit from behavioural biases is to buy on valuation differences and pre-commit not to sell on the short term, no matter how compelling the desire is to do so. Few fund managers have the courage to do this, and few fund managers can really profit from these strategies.

Have you any comments on the recent work by Andrew Lo (2004) on evolutionary dynamics as applied to the market place? Apart from the adaptive markets hypothesis are there any other new frameworks being developed?

Professor Lo is a good friend and colleague, and I have great respect for his work. His adaptive markets hypothesis is undoubtedly true. I was the editor who handled his first major assault on the EMH.[12]

His view then that the EMH was captured by a rigid and somewhat simplistic random walk hypothesis he now views to be somewhat extreme, and he now espouses an evolutionary view that posits that markets evolve in a behaviourally adaptive way. However, at every

---

11 Ross, S, 2004, *Neoclassical Finance*, Princeton University Press, Princeton.

12 Lo, A, and AC Mackinlay, 1988, "Stock market prices do not follow random walks: evidence from a simple specification test", *Review of Financial Studies 1*, 41–66.

step along the way behavioural biases will imply profit opportunities. To this extent, his views are unexceptionable. It is true that there has been tremendous innovation in the capital markets. Indeed, I tend to believe that this innovation has had and will have as profound an impact on the world economy as the growth of railroads and the resulting expansion of the steel industry had in the nineteenth century. New Carnegies and Rockefellers have come to the fore, and the hedge fund industry will generate new dynasties that will last to the fifth generation. But is this innovation a cause or effect of these new profit opportunities opening up? Silicon is the new steel, and the development and spread of information technology has at least as important a role to play in this financial innovation as has the profit opportunities that this innovation has given rise to.

In terms of fundamental strategic research, which areas do you think institutional investors should focus on? For example, strategic asset allocation (beta), security selection (alpha), new beta markets (for example, alternatives), TAA, portfolio construction (the MPT, PMPT)[13]**, risk management, etc.**

While many in the funds management business are intrigued by academic studies of anomalies, this literature troubles academics because anomalies by very definition constitute what we cannot explain. This is really at the heart of the current interest in behavioural finance, a hope that this structure will give us understanding of what is otherwise inexplicable.

There is much that we don't understand, and the job of academics is to try to give form and function to this understanding. *While much of the attention among practitioners has been the application of these new theories to the possibility of generating excess return, a neglected area is that of risk management.* Here, the newest literature on behavioural finance tells us something very disturbing. Loss averse trading patterns (also known as doubling down) are a characteristic of behavioural

---

13 Interestingly enough, Markowitz himself at some stage suggested that a model based on the semi-variance might be preferable. Recent advances in portfolio and financial theory, coupled with today's computing power, have led to a number of expanded risk/return paradigms also known as post–modern portfolio theory, or PMPT, focusing on downside risk using semi-variance and Sortino. Thus, MPT becomes a (symmetrical) special case of PMPT; see Rom and Ferguson (1993). Note that this proposed framework does not have any relationship with the PMPT alternative introduced by Ray Dalio earlier in our book, which diversifies among risk-adjusted betas (although coincidentally, the two theories bear the same name).

trading that can magnify potential downside risk, and may in fact be a complete explanation of recent rogue trading episodes.[14]

We do not blame the tiger for stalking its prey. But we do blame the zookeeper for leaving the cage door open. Recent academic findings suggest that there may be a rational explanation for the failures of supervision evident in the Australian Prudential Regulation Authority report and PriceWaterhouseCoopers' reports on the National Australia Bank currency desk problems of 2004, and of the findings of the 1995 Bank of England report on the Barings disaster.

One of the most profoundly important new papers circulating today is the work by Goetzmann and others on the development of manipulation-proof performance measures.[15] This is a very scary paper, a must-read by all serious institutional investors. While written in a technical language, the implications are very clear. By constructing a portfolio whose returns are concave to benchmark (for example an LTCM-style short volatility strategy implemented by buying units of the benchmark and writing out-of-the-money uncovered calls and puts), any money manager can generate a Sharpe ratio superior to that of the benchmark without employing any skill whatsoever. If we then allow the manager to leverage this portfolio, the alpha will be positive, limited only to the amount of margin he or she is allowed. They show that all performance measures are subject to the same problem, including more recent proposals, such as the Sortino ratio. The problem of course is that there is potentially unbounded downside risk, particularly when the strategy is leveraged sufficiently.

What is frightening is that this research suggests that modern performance metrics set up a necessary conflict between a manager's supervision and the risk management team. The supervisor rewards the trader and is in turn rewarded on the basis of these performance measures. The risk management team is concerned about both downside risk due to these strategies, and operational risk that arises when the negative consequences of these strategies are obscured. A classic and extreme case of concave portfolio

---

14 Doubling down refers to the behavior of doubling the bet size when on a losing streak, rather than taking the more prudent approach of cutting losses.

15 Goetzmann, WN, Ingersoll Jr, JE, Spiegel, MI, and I Welch, "Portfolio performance manipulation and manipulation-proof performance measures", November 2004, Yale ICF Working Paper No. 02-08. Available at SSRN: http://ssrn.com/abstract=302815 or DOI: 10.2139/ssrn.302815.

strategies is the doubling-down strategies implicated in recent rogue trading episodes. I remember discussing this issue at a meeting in Melbourne in October 2003 where I met with the senior risk management teams from leading Australian financial institutions. I remember being taken to task by the representative from the National Australia Bank, who argued that they were immune from this problem because they employed sophisticated value at risk technology. My response, that value at risk without reference to trading behaviour was part of the problem, not part of the solution (because it gave supervision a false sense of security), was widely quoted in the Australian press subsequent to the rogue trading episode at that bank that was revealed in January 2004.

US foundations have attracted a lot of press coverage for their superior investment performance, much of which can be traced back to their early asset allocation decision to move into alternatives (private equity, hedge funds, etc.) and out of especially US fixed income and stocks. Many of the highest profile foundations are attached to leading universities. Do you think their superior performance is due to a more innovative culture or access to thought leadership emanating from the academic world? Or does it have more to do with the fact that they are less constrained than other institutional investors such as pension funds, or something else?

The foundation we hear most of is the Yale endowment. This foundation has an appetite for risk unusual among foundations in the United States. Kingman Brewster, the President of Yale back in the late 1960s, was a visionary who saw looming what he termed an educational deficit at that institution. The income from the endowment, conservatively managed, was insufficient to propel the University into first place in the sciences. He took heed of a Ford Foundation report that in the late 1960s argued that university endowments were being managed too conservatively, and proposed instead a "total return" approach to investing. As a consequence, the endowment was invested aggressively into a growth equity portfolio that had high returns for several years and at least one negative return. At that point, the University launched a Campaign for

Yale, and from the success of this endeavour, due in large part to the great wealth of its alumni population, learned that the downside risk of its high-risk strategy was of minimal consequence. Subsequently the fund – led from 1985 by David Swensen, a doctoral graduate from its own Economics Department – has maintained an unusually aggressive investment strategy which in the event has paid handsome dividends for the University. *Many foundations seek to emulate Yale's investment success, but few have the foundation resources sufficient to support its considerable appetite for risk.*

Of some concern is the move by many pension funds to emulate this model and seek high returns that would offset future pension fund costs. As with the case of the Yale endowment, they have a deep pocket to support them in the case of a significant downturn. But it is not clear that this deep pocket, the US Pension Benefit Guarantee Corporation, can in fact support US Treasury Bill risk, let alone the risk emanating from alternative investments and exotic investment strategies.

What do you see as the hallmark of a successful long-term institutional investor?

What I have learned in my experience is that one hallmark of a successful long-term investor is the strength, and indeed courage, to temper the seat-of-the-pants approach characteristic of fundamental research with the hard edge of quantitative analysis, to learn not merely from experience but also from first principles. Such an approach involves a commitment to allocate resources to ongoing research to continually upgrade their investment process. This is a characteristic of the very best institutional managers. Such managers are able to understand in a realistic way the reason why they have succeeded in the past, and to articulate a comprehensive and realistic statement of their investment process going forward into the future. Part of this process necessarily involves a periodic review to accommodate to changing markets and circumstances. Black box analyses or "trust me" key persons are a common feature of fund management failure.

Let's talk a bit about the topic of hedge funds and the state of the industry. You recently gave a testimony before the US House of Representatives Committee. Can you for our readers give a brief overview of

what you presented and its implications for the wider industry?[16]

I was originally invited to testify before the US Congress House Financial Services Committee hearing on Hedge Funds and Systemic Risk in the Financial Markets on the basis of my recent research on hedge fund operational risk and optimal disclosure.[17] However, the terms of reference expanded and I was asked to give my views on the status of the industry and my views on systemic and operational risk. *My main points were that contrary to popular perception, there is remarkable diversity among hedge funds.* The industry is loath to disclose any information at all about their activities and as a result many believe that hedge funds are a monolithic whole. The danger is of course that the sins of the few will be visited on the many. I observed that contrary to popular perception hedge funds actually reduce systemic risk by taking on risk that would otherwise fall on the banking system. They provide valuable diversification opportunities for institutional investors, and reduce liquidity risk in the markets by buying when no-one is willing to buy and selling when no-one is willing to sell. More information would certainly help. But does this detract from the due diligence of sophisticated investors? With colleagues I studied the recent controversial and ultimately unsuccessful SEC attempt to increase hedge fund disclosure. We examined disclosures filed by many hedge funds in February 2006. I explained that leverage and ownership structures as of December 2005 suggest that lenders and hedge fund equity investors were already aware of hedge fund operational risk revealed in these forms. However, operational risk does not mediate the naive tendency of investors to chase past returns. Investors either lack this information, or regard it as immaterial. I concluded by emphasising the importance of selective disclosure. There is no need to know proprietary trading information, and the industry (or at least their representatives, the Managed Fund Association in the US) has now come to the view that by being more forthcoming they can allay public concern about systemic risk and operational risk.

---

16 "Hedge funds and systemic risk in the financial markets", hearing held on 13 March 2007.

17 Brown, SJ, Goetzmann, WN, Liang, B, and C Schwarz, "Optimal disclosure and operational risk: evidence from hedge fund registration", 7 January 2007. Yale ICF Working Paper No. 06-15, Available at SSRN: http://ssrn.com/abstract=918461.

What do you see as the main areas of academic research into the hedge fund industry at the moment? Is it all about the cloning and alternative beta (for example, Kat, Lo, Jaeger, Ibbotson) or is something else emerging?

I can really only talk about my own research. I think we have put a stake in the heart of the myth of market neutrality. *Zero beta is not a strategy but is rather the outcome of an investment strategy. Playing the slot machines is a zero beta investment strategy but is not by that fact desirable or particularly low risk.* I am fascinated by the idea that we might be able for the first time to develop a quantitative measure of operational risk, a measure which seems to explain the pattern of lending to hedge funds. I am also involved in new research on the measurement and management of tail risk.

Hedge funds are often blamed for volatility such as that which occurred during the Asia currency crisis of 1997–98. You wrote a paper in 1998 in which you argued that there was no empirical evidence that hedge fund managers were responsible. We all know that many famous hedge fund managers (such as Niederhoffer, Merriwether) lost tons of money during that crisis. Have you any insight as to who was on the other side of their trades? Who was responsible for that volatility? Are there any lessons from that experience which remain valid today or has the market already evolved too much?

My evidence seems to show that while Soros and other currency traders lost significant sums during that period it is not clear in the data which trades lost the most money. My data seems to show that many hedge funds had unwound their currency positions before the crisis. There was currency flight during that period, but at least in the Malaysian case it seems to be domestic in origin. A reading of the Australian financial press during the period of the crisis reveals that many Malaysian property trusts were heavily investing in Australian urban real estate at the very height of the crisis.[18] The most interesting aspect of this whole story was the credence given the views of Mahathir bin Mohamad, who argued in the pages of the *Wall Street Journal* (23 September 1997) that Soros was responsible

---

18 Brown, S, "Hedge funds: omniscient or just plain wrong", *Pacific-Basin Finance Journal* 9 2001 301-311.

for the crisis. He provided no evidence for this position, and there was in fact no evidence at all to support it. Soros was in fact famous as a currency trader for having bet and won $3.2 billion that the European Rate Mechanism would not hold in 1992. According to press accounts at the time, the counterparty to that trade was in fact a major Malaysian financial institution!

I notice that you're also on the board of the *Pacific-Basin Finance Journal*. What are some of the topics, academic and other, that attract your interest in the Asian region?

I am fascinated by the institutional differences in the markets and what we may learn from them. My most important published research on this topic relates to the reported underperformance of Japanese unit trust companies.[19] We found that this underperformance could be almost entirely attributed to the onerous and idiosyncratic tax environment under which Japanese unit trust companies were forced to operate. This paper was cited in the Japanese parliamentary discussions that led to a major revision in the unit trust tax code.

As you grew up in Australia, but have since moved to the US, I'd like to ask you a question on how the two compare. In general, I find the extent of financial innovation and even the quality of intellectual capital available in the Australian investment community to be high, especially given the small size of our economy.[20] A lot of foreign visitors comment on how far ahead we are in terms of industry developments such as sophistication of pension scheme investment management, retail platform distributions and preparedness to embrace new products. And yet much of the innovation occurring in the northern hemisphere as a result of the liability-driven investment trend is passing Australia by because of the different liability structure here. How would you compare Australia to the US, since you've worked in both?

---

19 Brown, S, with Goetzmann, W, Hiraki, T, Otsuki, T and N Shiraishi, "The Japanese open end fund puzzle", *Journal of Business* 74 2001 59-77.

20 This could potentially reflect the number of immigrants, as there's lots of technology transfer and entrepreneurs. For example, Australia is by some considered the hedge fund capital of Asia, in terms of assets managed, beating even centres such as Hong Kong, London and New York. Australia has also won a large number of the AsiaHedge awards.

I would definitely second the view that the quality of Australian intellectual capital is very high, and is much valued both in industry and in academic circles, particularly in the areas of finance and accounting. Australians are in high demand both on Wall Street and as PhD students in top tier US academic institutions.

There are differences in focus that have a substantial basis in the historical development of the two markets. Institutions in the United States are very focused on their fiduciary responsibilities. In the first instance, this was a result of ERISA legislation that governs private pension plans. Of recent interest is the Prudent Investor Law of New York passed in 1995 and which has spread across the United States, which reinforces the primary duties of fiduciaries, their responsibilities and potential liability. This focus has led to a major emphasis on risk management and technology to support this area.

The weight of the tax burden in Australia has focused attention here much more on tax-efficient investing, a focus many in the United States find interesting and indeed a little curious, as tax issues are a little more straightforward in the US.

Finally, the influence of accounting is far greater in Australia than in the US and this has influenced academic research to a much greater extent. Finance as an academic discipline here has branched out as a sub-discipline of accounting, where in the United States it is more often perceived as a branch of economics. This also leads to a different focus in terms of research interests.

What new academic research projects are you working on at the moment?

I am working on a number of projects both in the US and with Australian researchers. However, the most important research is the work I have done on optimal disclosure and hedge fund operational risk.[21] Required disclosure is a regulatory tool intended to allow market participants to assess manager risks without constraining manager actions. We use the recent controversial and ultimately unsuccessful SEC attempt to increase hedge fund disclosure to examine the value of disclosure to investors. By examining SEC

---

21 Brown, SJ, Goetzmann, WN, Liang, B and C Schwarz, "optimal disclosure and operational risk: evidence from hedge fund registration", 7 January 2007, Yale ICF Working Paper No. 06-15.

mandated disclosures filed by a large number of hedge funds in February 2006, we are able to construct a measure of operational risk distinct from market risk. Leverage and ownership structures as of December 2005 suggest that lenders and hedge fund equity investors were already aware of hedge fund operational risk characteristics. However, operational risk does not seem to mediate the naive tendency of investors to chase past returns, suggesting that investors either lack this information, or they do not regard it as material. These findings suggest that any consideration of disclosure requirements should take into account the endogenous production of information within the industry, and the marginal benefit of required disclosure on different investment clienteles.

What got you interested in finance in the first place? If not this, what would you have done?

My father was an accountant and company secretary in Melbourne and was fascinated by finance and the working of the markets. I had resisted this for many years. I had an outstanding economics training at Monash and had gone from there to the PhD program at the University of Chicago in 1972. I had no choice. I went there to study urban economics and econometrics which is where I may have ended up. However, there was such an intellectual ferment in the area of financial economics that I quickly shifted my interests in that direction. My first job was as a research scientist at Bell Telephone Laboratories, one of about 120 PhDs. I was hired as a research economist, but while there discovered the AT&T's pension plan, which became the major focus of my consulting activities within the company. The academic focus and industry exposure were very strong factors in my intellectual development.

What keeps you busy outside of office hours?

The most challenging thing I am doing at the moment is singing in a chamber choir. It's community based. They recently went for a tour to Ireland. Unfortunately, I couldn't make it or I would have had to disappoint 200 of my students. I like to spend time with my family too.

How do you see the investment industry in 10 years time?

Investment technology is changing with great speed, led by cutting-edge hedge funds like Renaissance Technologies. Cyber trading is replacing the trading desk, and humans are being taken out of the investment process at the high end. There will always be small traders, but the easy money is gone. I am convinced that without appropriate checks and balances these machines can go awry, and that there will always be an important role for human judgement. The most successful funds will be those which learn to integrate these machine-based systems with seat-of-the-pants checks and balances that can most effectively introduce common sense into the process.

Finally – investment: art, science or skill?

As my previous response indicates, I am convinced investment is both art and science. The proper balance is what I might term skill.

Conclusions

Stephen is among the most cited academics in the world. A few things sprang out of the interview:

- The academic literature on behavioural finance is very convincing. Yet, the problems with implementing behavioural finance are often underestimated. As Stephen mentions, it is about believing that "everybody but me is mad". Though the anomalies found may be beautiful and true, like Odysseus in the Odyssey, one can still try to wreck the ship. Of course, there are some successful exceptions.

- Many of the behavioural stories while plausible by themselves need to be shown to work together to explain asset prices. Many of the brightest people in the US are working to meet this challenge.

- Stephen took great care to explain the increased research focus on risk management, and especially the work by Goetzmann et al (2004) on Portfolio performance manipulation. He made clear why oft used measures such as Sharpe or Sortino may be deemed insufficient to model the derivatives nowadays used in (hedge) funds. We have re-sketched below one of the diagrams he drew for us during the interview.

Figure 1: The impact of selling options on Sharpe ratios

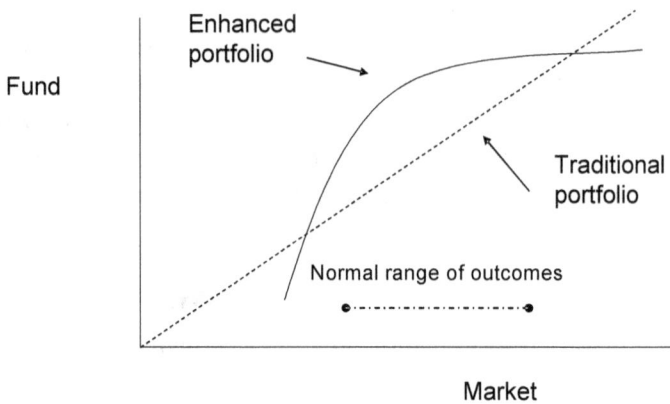

A traditional portfolio will fluctuate with a 1:1 relationship with the market (as represented by the dotted line, with a 45-degree angle). However, by passively adding derivatives (in this case, selling uncovered calls and puts) we can see that for a range of market outcomes (the "normal" range) the portfolio returns are enhanced, at the expense of tail risk. Hence we have a concave outcome. It is clear that the enhanced portfolio has a Sharpe ratio superior to the normal fund under the range of normal outcomes. The alpha can in fact be leveraged up, so in that sense, there is unlimited alpha. Stephen emphasises that this is exactly the way many hedge funds operate; by using leverage and assuming tail risk which is not captured in the traditional ratios, they deliver superior Sharpe ratios.[22]

- Similarly *portfolio insurance* can be deemed to have lower Sharpe ratios under normal circumstances, as we're now taking on the convex diagram, or the opposite side of the trade, whereby we cover off tail risk. This is in contrast to popular thinking whereby portfolio insurance is deemed useful to help improve short-term performance.

---

22 The fact that they are deemed "market neutral" does not impress him. He mentions one case he remembers where the client invested in a market neutral fund, the market didn't move anything, and yet the client lost everything. In the strict sense of the word, the fund was indeed "market neutral". As Stephen mentions, it could have made a one-way bet on the winner of the Superbowl as a legitimate market neutral action.

Figure 2: The impact of buying portfolio insurance on Sharpe ratios

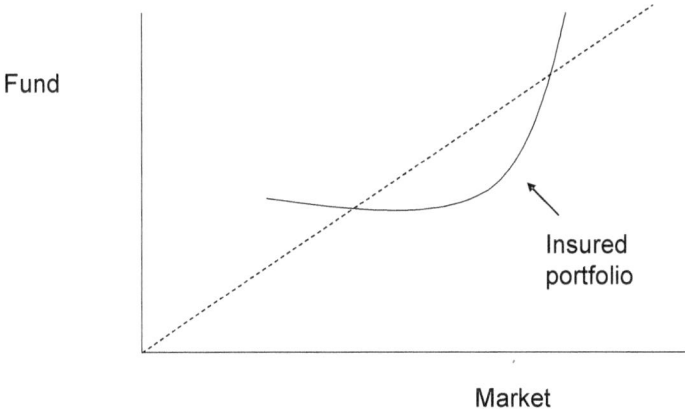

- Academics play a very important role in the investment management industry, as they provide fresh and sometimes completely different perspectives. As Stephen mentions, beware of the people who can successfully combine book-smart and street-smart, as the new breed of cyber traders don't sleep, don't have tantrums and never confuse buy and sell orders. Investment technology is changing with great speed, and cyber trading is replacing the trading desk. Humans are being taken out of the investment process at the high end. There will always be small traders, but the easy money is gone.

- There will always be an important role for human judgement. The most successful funds will be those which learn to integrate these machine-based systems with seat-of-the-pants checks and balances that can most effectively introduce common sense into the process.

13. Summary

> "Alchemy may be compared to the man who told his sons he had left the gold buried somewhere in his vineyard; where they by digging found no gold, but by turning up the mould, about the roots of their vines, procured a plentiful vintage. So the search and endeavours to make gold have brought many useful inventions and instructive experiments to light."
> – Francis Bacon (1561–1626)

For the past twelve chapters we have interviewed leading thinkers on many aspects of active management and engaged them on the alpha debate. Rather than seeking to cover all aspects of this broad topic, we focused on some of the central questions in the minds of many institutional investors.

THEMES

Several themes have emerged from the interviews.

1) Active versus passive – the moving frontier

As a first theme, the active versus passive debate remains alive and well, but has now moved into the hedge fund space, where returns previously regarded as alpha are being dissected into newly found beta factors. As more and more of what was once deemed "insight" becomes systemised, pure alpha may indeed become rare.

"Investing is a learned skill, in that there are lessons that must be experienced to really understand. Investing is not a science like physics where laws last forever. *In investing what you can hope to understand is what mistakes are being made and how long they will last.* You should not be overconfident when you find behavioural finance anomalies such as small caps or value." – Ben Inker

"Skill can also be thought of as 'divine inspiration'. It's a finite commodity, as in any skill-based game, it's a zero-sum game. Therefore, alpha you take away from the competition. After fees it's negative sum. It's always difficult to disentangle alpha and beta because we have not uncovered all the betas yet. After the APT, we've discovered additional factors such as small cap, dividend yield, or value versus growth. As the world evolves, we become more knowledgeable." – Stan Beckers

"Investment technology is changing with great speed, led by cutting-edge hedge funds. There will always be an important role for human judgment. The most successful funds will be those which learn to integrate these machine-based systems with seat-of-the-pants checks and balances that can most effectively introduce common sense into the process." – Stephen Brown

2) The future of the investment industry – the dual world

As to our second theme, how fund management firms are positioning themselves for the coming decade, here are some words of wisdom from our industry leaders:

"The investment business will consist of alpha generators and beta replicators (and firms that do both), and the alpha generators will have very smart people who understand financial engineering and are equipped with fabulous information technology. The amount of money firms will expend in the competition to produce alpha, and the levels of sophistication that these will produce, will be commensurate with the fees that they earn, which will increasingly differentiate between the various gradations of quality. In others words, the quality of play will increase dramatically." – Ray Dalio

"If the segmentation of the business (alpha/beta) is going to happen, then most active managers will gradually transition into pure alpha (or hedge funds). If that evolution is going to take place, the number of hedge funds could go up into tens of thousands. The proliferation in ETFs, and the more exotic ones, means that most conceivable risk premia can now be traded as ETFs. So, access to risk premia has now become cheap. The man in the street can buy into asset classes we didn't even know existed a couple of

years ago. ETFs accelerate the restructuring of the industry into beta and alpha providers. ETFs support a real paradigm shift."
– Stan Beckers

"Ten years ago, we would have said that a decade from now indexing would be a much larger portion of the market, and investors would look to active managers to provide alpha in a fairly pure way. With the benefit of hindsight, we can say that the world did move in that direction, but with much less speed than we thought. Ten years from now, we would expect the same trends to continue. If we are correct and the next ten years are also characterised by generally low, and fairly similar, returns across asset classes, we may see something of a shift among institutions to look more to finding managers they believe have alpha and concern themselves less with what asset class they happen to invest in to achieve that alpha."
– Ben Inker

"Some very large managers may have a harder time delivering alpha so we may see some additions to the industry leaders. I see more long short, alpha mandates, LDI mandates, more global mandates and global investors." – Jae Park

3) Generalist versus specialist – a place for both

A third theme that has emerged concerns how the industry will strive to tackle the generalist versus specialist debate. Again, the traditional debate has now moved into hedge fund space with many investors comparing the merits of the fund of funds versus the multi-strategy approach. One could mount a reasonable case for either the fund of funds or the multi-strategy approach to thrive most going forward, depending on the marginal cost of acquiring alpha externally or developing it internally.

"Multi-strategy has the advantages of fees and fee netting. Based on that distinction alone, multi-strategy will have an advantage. But that pre-supposes that multi-strategy managers have a comparative advantage across a broad range of various strategies. This is rare. Most multi-strategy funds will have their generic roots in a single strategy. To maintain alpha they have bolted on equity, fixed interest or volatility trading without necessarily having advantages in them. Another possible disadvantage of multi-strategy funds is that they have single-manager (operational) risk. Funds of funds have the comparative advantages of potentially being more broadly diversified and being able to choose the best of the breed. I believe both can play a meaningful role assuming they play on their strengths." – Stan Beckers

"Multi-strategy firms sit between single-strategy and fund of funds on the risk spectrum. The strategies they employ aren't as large in number or as diverse in nature as in a fund of funds, and you still have the business risk of an organisational collapse or a failure in risk management. So yes the returns of a multi-strategy can sometimes exceed a diversified fund of funds, but you're also accepting a higher level of risk than a diversified fund of funds. Multi-strategy managers are in essence just a collection of single-strategy managers owned by one firm, and the advantage is that a multi-strategy manager can allocate capital quickly between them. The problem is that the quality of each single-strategy team can vary, and the best traders often want to leave and start their own funds." – Blaine Tomlinson

In summary, multi-strategy funds offer a number of benefits over fund of funds, such as:

- Having greater agility in allocating capital across asset classes, strategies and up and down the capital structure.

- Avoiding the lock-ups of funds of funds.

- In general, having more proximity and depth of knowledge in the underlying strategies.

- Offering more transparency and liquidity, at lower fees.

- Having more equitable incentive fees: you can offset losses in one strategy versus gains in another.

- Easier verification of market neutrality.

But investors should remember that:

- The multi-strategy universe is very ill-defined, with lots of instruments, risk and return targets.

- Capacity is more often a limit than in funds of funds.

- All operational risk is with a single firm.

- There is a risk that a firm may have a strong house philoso-phy that will be reflected across all or most of the strategies employed, reducing actual diversification from expected levels.

This can be overcome by appointing several multi-strategy funds.

- Firms offering multi-strategy products face the problem of getting enough uncorrelated alpha sources. The cost of adding new alpha sources may be prohibitive, depending on the firm's origins.

- Funds of funds may have access to managers otherwise not available to new investors.

4) The current environment – concern and hope

A fourth theme is that a number of our experts are warning that the current low risk premium environment is not sustainable and that a major correction is likely (we note that part of this correction indeed occured a few months after the interviews were completed). Furthermore, with the increased opaqueness of the financial system, the power of central banks to act as last resort lender has somewhat diminished.

"The most striking thing about today's environment is that practically every risky asset looks overpriced. There have been other times in history when the headline equity indices have been more overvalued – 2000 is an obvious example – but we cannot find any previous time in history that such a broad swath of assets is simultaneously expensive. At current levels we believe all of the major sectors of the global equity markets are overpriced, credit spreads are universally too narrow, yield curves give too little premium for duration risk." – Ben Inker

"I think that the most analogous period to now was 1970–71, just before the Bretton Woods break-up, when Japan and Germany were in an analogous positions to China and India in that they were cheap and growing fast, running large balance of payments surpluses (while the US was running deficits) and the fixed exchange rate was being maintained via unsustainably large Japanese and German bond purchases of US bonds." – Ray Dalio

Still, there remains optimism on China and the emerging market story.

"The case for the overweight and underweight is straightforward. The US is the most expensive large market in the world, and most of Asia and emerging markets are significantly cheaper.

You don't have to have a particularly rosy view of the prospects for China or Asia generally in order to want to be in assets where they are cheaper. Adding in the fact that a number of these currencies are cheap and likely to appreciate versus the US dollar over the next seven years, and it is a case that more or less makes itself." – Ben Inker

"Yes I'm now bullish on emerging markets and currencies in anticipation of revaluations and the shift in wealth to developing nations, though I am more bullish on their currencies than their bonds and stocks. I even believe that the big balance of payments surplus countries' currencies will do well in a flight to quality, which is not typical." – Ray Dalio

"Many emerging markets have learned lessons from the Asian crisis. Countries have improved their foreign reserves and balance of payments positions dramatically, lowering their vulnerability to external shocks. Additionally, the implementation of financial, structural, social and economic reforms has benefited their economies. As such, markets are in a much stronger position today." – Mark Mobius

"In 1991 I made the prediction that the leadership of Asia, in economic and cultural terms, is passing to the Chinese. Part of it had to do with Japan being in deflation and turning inward. It did take some time for China and the Southeast Asian countries to become a major source of demand. I believe that we're somehow recreating the Ching dynasty's tributary system where foreign countries and businesses (such as Korea, Vietnam, Thailand, Burma and some Western countries now) are sending emissaries to China to pay tribute and do business again with the 'Middle Kingdom'." – Robert Lloyd George

5) The hedge fund industry – expecting a shakeout

A fifth theme is the increasing concern about the fast growing hedge fund industry.

"As a client recently said: there are about 8000 planes in the air and 100 good pilots." – Ray Dalio

"Do we need 10,000 managers? While having less managers might make it easier for those of us who select them, it also may mean less creativity and entrepreneurialism in hedge funds. There is a natural attrition rate in hedge funds. Only the best grow and

thrive over the long term. The lowest quality managers will inevitably close their funds and so will I suspect many average managers."
– Blaine Tomlinson

"I believe that the industry will go through a cycle where fees will have to be adjusted to meet performance standards. Successful funds may charge more than many of the low performers that will have to adjust their fees downward. This may lead to a flight of talent and an increased number of funds closing. Once this shakeout is complete, the percentage of manager-specific alpha in the industry might rise again." – Oliver Schupp

"My basic premise is that people invest in hedge funds looking for alpha. Unfortunately, in funds of funds, it turns out there are lots of betas embedded in the alpha. These are some of the more basic (or plain vanilla) betas as well, explaining 40% to 80% of fund of fund returns. So the hedge fund industry is far removed from being institutional quality, because people are not getting what it says on the label. Most hedge funds are not focused on delivering such a product, or any type of product that can justify their fees (on average)." – Stan Beckers

"The majority of back-testing shows that equity long/short and event-driven sector investing seemed easiest to replicate using regression modelling, while fixed-income arbitrage and equity market neutral tended to be more difficult to regress efficiently. It must be noted that there is no consensus on these findings and that depending on the methodologies applied and the factors chosen the results may significantly vary." – Oliver Schupp

"Hedge funds enhance portfolio returns at the expense of tail risk. Hence we have a concave outcome. It is clear that the enhanced portfolio has a Sharpe ratio superior to the normal fund under the range of normal outcomes. The alpha can in fact be leveraged up, so in that sense, there is unlimited alpha. Many hedge funds operate by using leverage and assuming tail risk which is not captured in the traditional ratios." – Stephen Brown

However, there are also some positive voices:

"Alpha returns may come down as more money enters the hedge fund industry. There are two views on this: the first that there will be an increasing number of unskilled managers providing the meat for the skilled managers. The second is that there is an increase in skilled managers and alpha may come down. The

2020 VISION: INVESTMENT WISDOM FOR TOMORROW

answer may lie in between. Our empirical observations note that the number of skilled managers is increasing; for example, from prop desks, or number two people raising capital. As Mark Twain used to say: 'Rumours of my demise are greatly exaggerated.' I think 2% alpha can be achieved, and does not seem like a high hurdle, whereas 2% consistent alpha would rank you among the top quartile of active long-only managers." – Bruce Dresner

6) Ethical investing – the jury is still out

A sixth theme is that SRI is going mainstream, whereas investors over the past decade mainly focused on the governance bit, with lots of shareholder engagement. The attention given to the E&S part has been very scarce until two or three years ago.

The UN PRI have been very beneficial to the industry as a whole, and the sustainability theme is becoming more and more integrated into investment processes and policies in one way or another, although the alpha benefit remains unproven in academic circles.

"In essence there are three competing hypotheses:

- *Extra-financial information is relevant.* We did some research (*Financial Analysts Journal*, 2005) and we found that eco-efficiency and high corporate governance did confirm hypothesis 1.

- *Extra-financial information is not relevant.* There are also studies on SRI mutual funds (including one of my own!) that show no differences relative to conventional funds.

- *Extra-financial information is relevant, but in a negative manner.* There are articles that mention that there is a 'price for sin'. That is, there is an extra return for the risk premiums you run for investing in, for example, defence and tobacco stocks.

To make things confusing, you can actually find academic evidence for all three hypotheses." – Rob Bauer

The likely impact of SRI is described by Rob as follows:

"Well, you probably would like to distinguish between long-term investors such as pension funds and insurance companies and short-term companies such as hedge funds. For long-term investors, for example, not accounting for climate change may lead to poor returns in the long run. There will be higher uncertainty, which will increase the discount rate in the long run.

For short-term investors, if prices have not reflected all this, you might want to take advantage of this. For example, there are more and more hedge funds emerging with an SRI theme."

7) Investing – art, science or skill?

A seventh theme is that despite all the emphasis on quantitative techniques, at the heart of superior performance lies human insight. Given the current available resources, the scope for sophisticated analysis is enormous. In that sense, science is a useful tool to help us develop ideas and make the most of them in the markets. Insight, focus and passion will continue to make the difference however.

"Investing has aspects of art, in that there is not, and will never be, a set of equations that allow you to consistently outperform – even if such equations could be found, their very use would change the landscape so that they ceased to work. Imagination and creativity will always be required to outperform, even for quantitative investors." – Ben Inker

"There is a scientific method to it all, but it is the art that makes us humans indispensable, as we need to process information and be one step ahead of our opponents. So, yes although there are very useful quantitative approaches, I'm not a believer in a generalised pure quant approach." – Jae Loomis

"Does the edge lie in being a quant or fundamentalist? They are probably the same, as at the heart of a good quant process will be fundamental insight. Otherwise we revert to data mining." – Stan Beckers

"There are all sorts of ways to make money in the markets. However, I believe that the best way, and the way that increased competition will drive investing toward, is art and skill systemised into science." – Ray Dalio

"I've always felt the key to successful investing is the ability to adapt to change. Typically this also means focusing one's efforts on areas that are less travelled. So the more inefficient the asset class, the more art and skill is required." – Bruce Dresner

"To make the distinction between art and science is unhealthy. People always like to look at things in a binary fashion. If you understand statistics, you'd know there are many more things between 0 and 1. It is true though, that in the sixties investing was more of an art. In fact you'd be likely to have a degree in history or such. Today, with all the available computing power, it's leaning more towards science." – David Harding

For all the science involved, passion is still rated as among one of the essential factors.

"What keeps me motivated is the 'love of the game', which started as a teenager trading stocks and commodities. Although I no longer sit on the trading floor, I still like passing orders, and love figuring out strategies of what to buy and when. Passion and the drive to excel are the most important attributes to succeed in the business." – Ray Dalio

"I've toured rubber plantations in Thailand and road-tested bikes over the pothole-ridden roads of rural China. I've choked on roasted camel's meat, sheep's eyeball, guinea pig and dined (surprisingly well) on scorpions on toast, all to find undervalued companies before other investors do. I think you could safely say that I'm driven." – Mark Mobius

14. EVOLUTIONARY DYNAMICS IN THE MARKETPLACE

"It is not from the benevolence of the butcher, the brewer, or the baker that we expect our dinner, but from their regard to their own interest."
– Adam Smith (1723–1790)

So far, in our book we have focused on alpha mainly through the different asset classes. It is now time to examine the broader evolutionary perspective. In this section, we will examine some of the recent academic thinking into how evolutionary dynamics may help improve our understanding of the financial markets and the transformation of alpha.

As Stephen Brown mentioned, "many of the behavioural stories while plausible by themselves need to be shown to work together to explain asset prices. Many of the brightest people in the US are working to meet this challenge."

To bring it all together, in recent times leading academics such as Andrew Lo (2004) have been working on theories of *evolutionary dynamics* to put together a more coherent paradigm. Much of what behavioural finance cites as counterexamples to economic rationality – for example, loss aversion, overconfidence, overreaction, mental accounting, and other behavioural biases – which can possibly offer opportunities for alpha generation are, in fact, consistent with an evolutionary model of individuals adapting to a changing environment via simple heuristics.[1] Andrew Lo's *adaptive markets hypothesis (AMH)* consists of the following components:

---

1 This approach is heavily influenced by recent advances in the emerging discipline of evolutionary psychology, which builds on the seminal research of Wilson (1975).

- Individuals act in their own self-interest.

- Individuals make mistakes.

- Individuals learn and adapt.

- Competition drives adaptation and innovation.

- Natural selection shapes market ecology.

- Evolution determines market dynamics.

Specifically, the adaptive markets hypothesis can be viewed as a new version of the EMH, derived from evolutionary principles.

"Prices reflect as much information as dictated by the combination of environmental conditions and the number and nature of species."[2] – Andrew Lo

If multiple species (or the members of a single highly populous species) are competing for rather scarce resources within a single market, that market is likely to be highly efficient; for example, the US stock market, as compared to, say, emerging markets or some of the more exotic private markets. One of the conclusions that can be reasonably drawn from the AMH is that *alpha is at least to some extent cyclical in nature*, a view supported by some of our participants.

> *"The inefficiencies in the market are highly cyclical and will vary through time. If we think about alpha as what the skilled players take from the unskilled, then the supply of unskilled players is important. There is a need for a constant supply. The skill level I find to be much higher than, say, a decade ago. So it's difficult to put a number on it. But we know that double-digit alphas are rare and usually unsustainable to the extent that people that are skilful will have difficulty in maintaining that edge."*

– Stan Beckers

The concept of bounded rationality

Another argument for the persistence of alpha may trace its origins to Simon (1955), who introduced the concept of bounded rationality, suggesting that individuals are incapable of the rational behaviour and optimisation that neoclassical economics assumes.

---

2   Species may refer to a certain group of investors who share similar attributes; for example, portfolio managers, traders, arbitrageurs, central banks or pension funds.

As optimisation is costly and humans are limited in their computational abilities, they engage in "satisficing", an alternative to optimising in which individuals make choices that are satisfactory, but not necessarily optimal. Individuals make choices based on past experience and their best guess as to what might be optimal, and they learn by receiving positive or negative reinforcement from the outcomes. If they receive no such reinforcement, they do not learn.

Reconsider the following quote by Ben Inker:

> *"Many times, market inefficiencies are set due to the way people are paid; that is, there is a lot of career risk at stake which is due to the agency problem. Although incentive fees and co-investing may help a bit, I haven't figured out the perfect structure for incentives yet."*

In this case, it is no surprise that many fund managers are in fact not optimising investment returns, but are rather minimising career risk, as a result of the environment they operate in. Rather than labelling such behaviour as irrational it should be recognised that sub-optimal behaviour is not unlikely when we take heuristics out of their evolutionary context. A more accurate term for such behaviour might be "maladaptive".

As Andrew Lo puts it, "the flopping of a fish on dry land may seem strange and unproductive, but under water, the same motions are capable of propelling the fish away from its predators."

Market efficiency is context-dependent and dynamic, depending on the seasons, the number of predators and prey, and the ability to adapt to an ever-changing environment. The more resources present, the less fierce the competition. As competition increases, either because of dwindling food supplies or an increase in the animal population, resources are depleted which, in turn, causes a population decline eventually, decreasing the level of competition and starting the cycle again. In some cases cycles converge to corner solutions; that is, certain species become extinct, food sources are permanently exhausted, or environmental conditions shift dramatically. By viewing economic profits as the ultimate food source on which market participants depend for their survival, the dynamics of market interactions and financial innovation can be readily derived. This applies to long-only and hedge fund managers alike.

"We strongly believe that one of the major benefits of investing in hedge funds is the ability of managers to adapt to changing macroeconomic conditions. When there is new information, they adapt their thinking. One final observation I'll share is that longer term, the overall hedge fund opportunity set is best when you have high levels of government intervention, corporate activity and investor inefficiency."

– Blaine Tomlinson

Practical implications

From the evolutionary dynamics model presented, a number of implications can be derived for investors (Lo, 2004):

- *The relation between risk and reward exists, but is unlikely to be stable over time.* Such a relation is determined by the relative sizes and preferences of various populations in the market ecology, as well as institutional aspects such as the regulatory environment and tax laws.

- *In contrast to the classical EMH, arbitrage opportunities do exist from time to time.* As Grossman and Stiglitz (1980) observed, without such opportunities, there will be no incentive to gather information, and the price-discovery aspect of financial markets will collapse. From an evolutionary perspective, the existence of active liquid financial markets implies that profit opportunities must be present. As they are exploited, they disappear. But new opportunities are also continually being created as certain species die out, as others are born, and as institutions and business conditions change.

- *Investment strategies will wax and wane, performing well in certain environments and performing poorly in other environments.* Contrary to the classical EMH in which arbitrage opportunities are competed away, eventually eliminating the profitability of the strategy designed to exploit the arbitrage, the AMH implies that such strategies may decline for a time and then return to profitability when environmental conditions become more conducive to such trades.

- *Innovation is the key to survival.* The classical **EMH** suggests that certain levels of expected returns can be achieved simply by bearing a sufficient degree of risk. The AMH implies that the risk/reward relation varies through time, and that a better way of achieving a consistent level of expected returns is to adapt to changing market conditions.

- *Finally, the AMH has a clear implication for all financial market participants: survival is the only objective that matters.* While profit maximisation, utility maximisation, and general equilibrium are certainly relevant aspects of market ecology, the organising principle in determining the evolution of markets and financial technology is simply survival. *Even ideas are subject to "survival of the fittest".*

"In the past, from the point of thinking of a trading rule to testing it took a long time (to gather the data and test it), so that it was the exploration of a concept which bottlenecked my progress. Now, it's the opposite – the gathering and processing of the data is so fast that my intellectual ability to process the information is the bottleneck. The game of investing has gotten much more sophisticated since I started jotting my rules down on yellow pads."

– Ray Dalio

AFTERWORD

"The truth is rarely pure and never simple."
– Oscar Wilde (1854–1900)

Since the idea for this book first came about, the concept of alpha–beta separation has become more and more entrenched. But perhaps, as Bruce Dresner mentioned, in terms of the paradigm shift in the making, we're still at "the end of the beginning".

The academic and industry leaders who have contributed to this book have very different perspectives on the issues raised. But of course there is one perspective missing from the book, which is the view of time.

Evolution and life are all about change. Similarly active management and alpha generation are dynamic processes, and it is very likely that the questions in this book will produce very different answers if posed in a few years time, even if the interviewees are the same.

The book is therefore not meant to provide definitive answers as to what the investment world will look like by 2020, but can be used as a tool for deliberating upon what may happen to the industry within a certain context. Nevertheless, the following assumptions may be safely made:

- Transaction costs will come down as the number of derivative instruments increases.

- The skill of the average player will increase.

- Capital markets will become increasingly efficient.

- We will keep finding new betas that explain what was once presumed to be skill.

- The constantly changing nature of the demand and supply of alpha will increase the complexity of active management in the markets.

As the level of institutional investor education rises and investors better understand the factor exposures underlying their investment portfolios, alpha and beta will in due course be rewarded at their relevant pricing.

As a final word, in nature evolution is the exception, and extinction is the norm: something worth pondering when considering the alpha-producing capabilities of the *average* (hedge) fund manager.

Whatever role you're currently in, we hope that this book has helped your understanding of the major trends in the investment industry, and we would like to wish you all the best in your future investment endeavours.

About the author

Harry Liem is a Senior Associate with Mercer in Sydney, where he advises institutional and retail investors on asset allocation and manager selection decisions. He also undertakes specialist research on hedge funds and various strategic issues.

He has extensive industry experience working as a portfolio manager and strategist for a number of reputable companies in Europe, Asia and Australia, including ING, Perennial and Rabobank/Stroeve Investment Bank.

He is a regular speaker at conferences and has lectured on hedge funds, equity analysis and portfolio management for the Financial Services Institute of Australasia and the University of Technology, Sydney.

Harry holds a BSc and MSc in Computing Science from Delft University of Technology (the Netherlands), an MBA from Stirling University (UK) and is a Chartered Financial Analyst.

He resides in Sydney with his wife and two children.

References

1) Rethinking the investment ABC

____, 2006, The Asset Management Industry in 2010, McKinsey & Company.

____, May 2005, "New sources of return", JP Morgan Asset Management.

Cardarelli, R, and U Kenichi, April 2006, "Awash with cash, why are corporate savings so high?", *IMF World Economic Outlook*.

Chernoff, J, 14 June 2004, "Radical shift", *Pensions & Investments Magazine*.

Dalio, R, December 2005, "Engineering targeted returns and risks", Bridgewater.

Fromson, B, and D, June, 2000, "A cautionary tale from a big picture guy", TheStreet.com.

Hill, JM, August 2006, "Pension fund priorities: reorienting asset mix management to risk & strategy allocation", Goldman Sachs.

Ibbotson, RG, and P Chen, June 2005, "Sources of hedge funds returns: alphas, betas and costs", Yale ICF Working Paper No. 05-17.

Jenks, P, and S Eckett, 2002, *The Global-Investor Book of Investing Rules*, Harriman House.

Leib, B, October 2000, "The world according to Ray Dalio", *Derivatives Strategy*.

Liem, H, and D Timotijevic, November 2005, "Survival of the fittest – fund of hedge funds survey", Mercer Investment Consulting.

Ruffel, C, 5 July 2005, "A wind of change", *Plan Sponsor*.

Teitelbaum, R, January 2006, "Bridgewater's hunt for pensions", *Bloomberg Markets*.

To, HK, 26 April 2006, "The new financial order?", MarketThoughts.com.

Ward, S, July 2005, "Bipolar disorder: interview with Ray Dalio", *Barrons*.

2) The search for the holy grail

Amanti, G, Bowler, B, Davi, J, and H Ebens, 18 October 2006, "New alternatives in alternative investing", Merrill Lynch.

Beckers, S, Curds, R, and S Weinberger, September 2006, "Funds of hedge funds take the wrong risks", *Investment Insights*, Barclays Global Investors.

Dopfel, F, March 2005, "Waiter! What's this hedge fund doing in my soup?", *Investment Insights*, Barclays Global Investors.

Grinhold, RC, and RN Kahn, 1999, *Active Portfolio Management*, McGraw-Hill.

Hasanhodzic, J, and A Lo, August 2006, "Can hedge-fund returns be replicated?: The linear case", MIT.

Ibbotson, Roger G, and P Chen, June 2005, "Sources of hedge funds returns: alphas, betas and costs", Yale ICF Working Paper No. 05-17.

Jaeger, L, and C Wagner, 7 November 2005, "Factor modeling and benchmarking of hedge funds: can passive investment in hedge fund strategies deliver?", Partners Group.

Kat, HM, and HP Palaro, February 2007, "Replication based evaluation of hedge fund performance", Cass Business School, City University London.

Thomas, LR, February 2004, "Engineering an alpha engine", Pimco.

Williamson, C, 13 March 2006, "Alpha is called a finite commodity", InvestmentNews.com.

3) A brave new world

____, 2005, "New sources of return, major US pension plans search for higher performance", JP Morgan.

____, 1 November 2005, "Trends in institutional alternatives investing", Greenwich Associates.

Fama, EF, and GW Schwert, (1977), "Asset Returns and Inflation", *Journal of Financial Economics*.

Fowler, ML, October 2003, "All in the family", *Investment Advisor*.

Hatheway, L, Liew, K, Palma, J, and J Delaney, 10 February 2006, "Back to the future?", Weekly Weight Watcher, UBS.

Liem, H, March 2006, "Thinking alternative – trustees wake up to the new environment", Mercer Investment Consulting.

Liem, H, and M Utreja, January 2006, "China and India, rethinking the global economic balance", Mercer Investment Consulting.

Lord, M, April 2005, "Trends and issues 2005 NACUBO Endowment Forum: managers find pickings quite slim", TIAA-CREF Institute.

Lowenstein, R, 30 October 2005, "The end of pensions", *New York Times*.

4) The road less travelled

____, 5 November 2001, "Interview with Mark Mobius", Commanding Heights.

____, 12 June 2006, "Q&A: Mark Mobius on emerging markets", FT.com.

____, 4 July 2006, "Indian markets are still expensive: Mark Mobius", *The Hindu Business Line*.

Burton, D, Tseng, W, and K Kang, June 2006, "Asia's Winds of Change", *IMF Quarterly Magazine*.

Clifford, M, 11 May 1998, "Mark Mobius: global pioneer", *BusinessWeek*.

Gu, GZ, 27 January 2006, "Mark Mobius: the emerging markets nomad", *Asia Times*.

Hall, A, 27 September 1998, "Investment guru with the world on his shoulders", *Business Times South Africa*.

Hogg, A, 3 February 2006, "Interview with Mark Mobius", Moneyweb.

Lette, G, Liem, H, Stewart, G and J Thompson, September 2005, "A strategic tilt to equity markets in fast growing economies", Mercer Investment Consulting.

Mobius, M, 1996, *On Emerging Markets*, Pitman Publishing, London.

Mobius, M, 1999, *Passport to Profits*, Warner Books, London.

Scott, GC, March 2005, "Interview with Dr J. Mark Mobius", *The Scott Letter*.

5) The east west pendulum

Lette, G, Liem, H, Stewart, G, and J Thompson, September 2005, "A strategic tilt to equity markets in fast growing economies", Mercer Investment Consulting.

Liem, H, and M Utreja, 2006, "China and India – Rethinking the global economic balance", Mercer Investment Consulting.

Lloyd, GR, 1992, *The East West Pendulum*, Quorum books.

Lloyd, GR, 2005, *The East West Pendulum Revisited*, Lloyd George Management.

Rees-Mogg, W, 25 November 2005, "Buy Sung and Tang vases", The Daily Reckoning.

6) High yield or high grade?

Braddick, P, and A Montalti, May 2006, "Is credit growth sustainable?", ANZ Bank.

Cardarelli, R, and K Ueda, April 2006, "Awash with cash: why are corporate savings so high?", *IMF World Economic Outlook*.

Chancellor, E, 2005, *Crunch Time For Credit*, Harriman House, 2005.

Evans-Pritchard, A, 23 February 2006, "Global Credit Ocean Dries Up", *The Telegraph*.

Foster, JB, May 2006, "The Household debt bubble", Monthly Review, vol. 58, no.1.

Kindleberger, CP, 2000, *Manias, Panics, and Crashes: A History of Financial Crises*, Wiley.

King, M, and R Fumagalli, May 2006, "What might burst the credit bubble?", Citigroup.

7) Trends in the hedge fund industry

_____, 2007, *HFR Year End 2006 Industry report*, HFR.

Asness, C, 1998, "Market-neutral investing: putting the 'hedge' in 'hedge funds'", AQR Capital Management working paper.

Asness, C, Krail, R, and J Liew, 2001, "Do hedge funds hedge?" AQR Capital Management.

Beder, TS, Budhraja, V, De Figueiredo, R, and R Meredith, 2005, "How large could the hedge fund industry grow?", Citigroup.

Chen, P, and RG Ibbotson, 27 May 2005, "Sources of hedge funds returns", Ibbotson Associates.

Dalio, R, and J Rotenberg, 24 April 2006, "What a hedge fund bust would look like", Bridgewater Daily Observations.

Green, P, 2004. "Hedge fund investing across multiple states of the environment", Merrill Lynch.

Hutchings, W, 7 November 2005, "Tomlinson gets into his stride at FRM", *Financial News*.

Kabiller, D, O'Hara, J, Rosengarten, J and B Tomlinson, 1998, "Hedge funds demystified: their potential role in institutional portfolios", Goldman Sachs Pension and Endowment Forum.

Kahn, RN, Scanlan, MH, and LB Siegel, May 2006, "Five Myths about fees", *Barclays Investment Insights*, Volume 9, Issue 2.

Kuper, S, 11 August 1998, "Hedge funds now revealed as great for widows and orphans", *The Financial Times*.

8) The paradox of passive alpha

Amanti, G, Bowler, B, Davi, J, and H Ebens, 18 October 2006, "New alternatives in alternative investing", Merrill Lynch.

Beckers, S, Curds, R, and S Weinberger, September 2006, "Funds of hedge funds take the wrong risks", *Investment Insights*, Barclays Global Investors.

Hasanhodzic, J, and A Lo, August 2006, "Can hedge-fund returns be replicated?: the linear case", MIT.

Hill, JM, Mueller, B, and V Balasubramanian, 2 November 2004, "The 'secret sauce' of hedge fund investing – trading risk dynamically", Goldman Sachs.

Ibbotson, RG, and P Chen, June 2005, "Sources of hedge funds returns: alphas, betas and costs", Yale ICF Working Paper No. 05-17.

Jaeger, L, and C Wagner, 7 November 2005, "Factor modeling and benchmarking of hedge funds: can passive investment in hedge fund strategies deliver?", Partners Group.

Tomeo, J, Covino, R, and B Chun, June 2005, "Is indexing suitable for hedge fund investing?", *AIMA Journal*.

9) How portable is hedge fund skill?

Bensman, M, July/August 1996, "Moving alpha", *Derivatives Strategy*.

BlackRock Alternative Advisors, LP, January 2007, "Designing an alpha engine in theory and practice", *The Euromoney Portable Alpha Handbook 2007*.

Calio, V, October 2006, "No love for portable alpha", *Pensions and Investments*.

Custard, C, and L Tierney, April 2006, "Alpha transport in asset allocation", Schroders.

Custer, C, November 2005, "An introduction to portable alpha", SEI Investments.

Douin, F, 11 October 2004, "Portable alpha 101", JPMorgan Fleming.

Jacobs, BI and KN Levy, May 1999, "Alpha transport with derivatives", *Journal of Portfolio Management*, 25, 55-60.

Jones, C, August 2004, "Back to basics: portable alpha", *Pensions Management*.

Kung, E, B Capital and L Pohlman, Winter 2005, "An alpha + beta framework", *Journal of Investing*.

Michel, J, and S Foote, 15 October 2004, "Importing investment value added – alpha transport", Mercer Investment Consulting.

10) Is the trend still your friend?

Diz, F, 2001, "Understanding sources of CTA performance", BMFR.

Green, P, February 2004, "Hedge fund investing across multiple states of the environment", Merrill Lynch.

Kat, HM, November 2002, "Managed futures and hedge funds: a match made in heaven", City University London, Cass Business School.

Koomar, S, May 2004, "Managed futures can save your tail", KV1 Asset Management.

Liang, B, November 2003, "On the performance of alternative investments: CTAs, hedge funds and fund-of-funds", University of Massachusetts at Amherst, Isenberg School of Management.

Linter, J, May 1983, "The potential role of managed commodity futures accounts in portfolios of stocks and bonds", Harvard University.

Lungarella, G, 5 June 2006, "The case for managed futures", *MarHedge*.

Sott, KL, September 2004, "The blending of alternatives: adding CTAs to a portfolio of hedge funds", *AIMA Journal*.

11) Alpha in sustainable investing

_____, May 2007, "The challenges facing the world economy", Societe Generale.

Aziz, A, Goss, A, Milevsky, M, Thomson, J, and D Wheeler, Spring 2006, "Cleaning a passive index", *The Journal of Portfolio Management*.

Bauer, R, 7 December 2006, "Sustainable investing, luxury or necessity?", Netherlands Pensions Summit.

Blue, T, 23 September 2006, "Fair weather funds find new favour", *The Australian*.

Guenster, N, Derwall, J, Bauer, R, and K Koedijk, 25 July 2005, "The economic value of corporate eco-efficiency", Working Paper, Erasmus University.

Hoyle, S, 18 November 2006, "Changes on the road to sustainability: Al Gore", *Sydney Morning Herald*.

Hunt, PC, September 2006, "Value at risk revisited", Sustainable Development International.

Intergovernmental Panel on Climate Change (IPCC), February 2007, "Climate change: the physical science basis", United Nations.

Oliver, S, 26 October 2006, "Global warming – can't be ignored by investors" AMP Capital Investors.

Scott, M, 9 October 2006, "Finance: there is more to profit than the bottom line", *Financial Times*.

UNEP Finance Initiative and the UN Global Compact, April 2006, *Principles for Responsible Investment*, United Nations.

12) What's new in modern finance?

Brown, SJ, Goetzmann, WN, and A Kumar, 1998, "The Dow Theory: William Peter Hamilton's track record re-considered", *Journal of Finance*, 53, 1311-1333.

Brown, SJ, Goetzmann, WN, and B Liang, 2004, "Fees on fees in funds of funds", Yale ICF Working Paper No. 02-33.

Brown, SJ, Goetzmann, WN, and JM Park, 2000, "Hedge funds and the Asian currency crisis of 1997", *Journal of Portfolio Management*, 26, 95-101.

Cowles, A, 1933, "Can stock market forecasters forecast?", Econometrica 1, 309-325.

Fama, EF, 1970, "Efficient capital markets: a review of theory and empirical work", *Journal of Finance*, American Finance Association, vol. 25(2), 383-417, May.

Lakonishok, J, Shleifer, A, and RW Vishny, 1994, "Contrarian investment, extrapolation and risk", *Journal of Finance*, 49, 1541-1578.

Lo, AW, 2004, "The adaptive markets hypothesis: market efficiency from an evolutionary perspective", *Journal of Portfolio Management*, 30, 15-29.

Markowitz, H, 1952, "Portfolio selection", *Journal of Finance*, Vol. 7.

Rom, BM, and K Ferguson, 1993, "Post-modern portfolio theory comes of age", *Journal of Investing*.

Sharpe, WF, 1964, "Capital asset prices: a theory of market equilibrium under consideration of risk", *Journal of Finance*, vol. 19.

14) Evolutionary dynamics in the marketplace

Andrikopoulos, P, "Modern finance vs. behavioural finance: an overview of key concepts and major arguments".

Du, K, May 2004, "Efficient markets hypothesis and behavioural finance: a Kuhnian review", Peking University.

Fama, EF, May 1970, "Efficient capital markets: a review of theory and empirical work", *Journal of Finance, American Finance Association*, vol. 25(2), 383-417.

Grossman, S and J Stiglitz, 1980, "On the impossibility of informationally efficient markets", *American Economic Review*, 70, 393-408.

Lo, AW, 2004, "The adaptive markets hypothesis: market efficiency from an evolutionary perspective", *Journal of Portfolio Management*, 30, 15-29.

Shiller, RJ, October 2002, "From efficient market theory to behavioural finance", Cowles Foundation.

Simon, H, 1955, "A behavioural model of rational choice", *Quarterly Journal of Economics*, 69, 99-118.

Wilson, E, 1975, *Sociobiology: The New Synthesis*, Harvard University Press.

INDEX

www.ingramcontent.com/pod-product-compliance
Lightning Source LLC
Chambersburg PA
CBHW071202210326
41597CB00016B/1646